# HUNTER GATHER COOK

## HANDBOOK

### ADVENTURES IN WILD FOOD

## NICK WESTON

First published 2022 by Guild of Master
Craftsman Publications Ltd
Castle Place, 166 High Street, Lewes,
East Sussex, BN7 1XU, UK

This book was created using material from
*Hunter Gather Cook*, first published 2019.

ISBN 978 1 78494 633 3

Publisher   Jonathan Bailey
Production   Jim Bulley
Senior Project Editor   Dominique Page
Editors   Nicole Bator & Sara Harper
Managing Art Editor   Robin Shields
Illustrator   Paul Burley
Photographer   David Loftus

Colour origination by GMC Reprographics
Printed and bound in China.

# CONTENTS

# GATHER

# INTRODUCTION

What is Hunter Gather Cook? On paper, it's a cookery school, focusing on four basic elements: game, foraging, fire and cookery. But in reality, it is so much more than that. It is a place you learn about your food before it greets you on the table and a place that will give you a lifetime connection to the wild: how to observe it, nurture it, immerse yourself in it and cook it. There is no restaurant at HGC, just a treehouse and an old barn; there is no Wi-Fi; and there is no wine list. There is smoke, there is fire and fur and feather. Of course, technically, and grammatically, it should be Hunt Gather Cook or Hunter-Gatherer Cook. But it isn't and I'll blame my dyslexic brain for that.

IF HGC HAS A CORE, THEN FIRE IS IT. Our entire concept was originally based around this element. What it can do for food is astounding: the different stages at which it can be used from its most fierce to it most gentle is more versatile than any kitchen appliance that we know today. Fire cookery goes way beyond the barbecue and the garden is a great place to begin, be it a simple fire pit or something more elaborate, such as a clay oven or asador.

Hunting and gathering is at the forefront of what we do. There are vast swathes of flavours in the wild to rediscover and a bounty of incredible game to be appreciated. But it all has to be tied in with that which we are more used to. Vegetables, oils, vinegars, herbs and spices are all part of the larder at HGC as with any other kitchen. Vegetables and greens are just as important as meat. As a conscious omnivore, a varied diet is a healthy diet and vegetables take centre stage just as much as meat does. The way in which we build many of the dishes in this book start with what is in season in terms of game and wild, we then add what veg is available and works well with both the

aforementioned and then turn to the pantry for pickles and fermented food. But it still adheres to the formula I have always worked from and where ingredients slot in to make the perfect meal. There is a circle that exists in nature that is worth taking note of: the animals we hunt eat wild food and they live in the woods, fields and meadows where we forage all our ingredients. The woods give us fuel and fire and we cook both of them on fire from the woods. They end up on the plate in the very place they all once lived. If there is a key to fresh, local and seasonal than maybe this is it.

What HGC is designed to do is to educate and inspire. We live in a world that moves way too fast for any of us. To escape that and immerse yourself in the natural world, if only for a day, is food for thought. Learning how to identify and use wild plants, how to process a variety of wild game, how to make fire from scratch and how to cook on it are central to what we do. These are the things that make a plate of food have real meaning. There is adventure in wild food, there is a journey behind every wild ingredient and that's always the bit that tastes the best.

FIRE

"Above all else, fire has a wonderful ability to bring us all together to share, celebrate and enjoy the food that is cooked over it..."

# COOKING WITH FIRE

We have been cooking with fire for thousands of years. In the not-too-distant past, the hearth was central to every home. In many parts of the world it still is. Today the kitchen remains the hub of most households, although the hearth has been replaced with more sophisticated methods to cook our food. For many of us, cooking over fire is a summer activity strictly reserved for social gatherings when the sun is out. But cooking over fire doesn't have to be limited to that season. Winter barbecues are some of the most enjoyable: after all, what better time is there to be next to a fire?

MANY OF THE TECHNIQUES you're going to see in the following pages might seem out of reach, but I can assure you they are not. Even with the smallest of outdoor spaces, they can still be achieved. Many of them, along with most of the recipes in this book, can be recreated at home on a barbecue or in a wood-fired oven. But what if we want to take it a step further?

Fire cookery is a constantly evolving collaboration of methods from all over the world that can rub off on all of us. No other form of cookery lends itself to DIY like fire. I know people who have built hot smokers from old filing cabinets and fire pits from washing machine drums. My housemates and I once made a barbecue out of a shopping trolley at university. We don't all need to be expert metalworkers to create masterpieces: wire, chains, fixings and even freshly cut wood can all help us bodge together grills, asadors, skewers, skillets and spits. If you want to have something custom made that's going to stand the test of time, then there are fabricators out there that can do it for you.

But for now, let's strip it right back to ground level, which is where most of us first cooked on a fire. Although you can buy fire pits that will both look fancy and save a section of your lawn, a fire pit to me is literally a shallow hole in the ground, where a section of turf has been dug up

and with a load of bricks carefully placed around the edges to contain the fire. This is exactly what I have in my garden at home. I have a few barbecues too, but sometimes the simplicity of being sat on the grass over a small grill with wooden skewers dug into the grass suspended over coals resonates with me more. It's a gloriously simple way of cooking and takes me back to the first piece of food I cooked over fire as a child, a rather burnt sausage.

Sometimes, these simple holes in the ground can become more elaborate, and you can end up with what we have at our Treehouse: a full-on multi-platform fire cookery cathedral with built-in cold smoker, clay oven and wood store. It certainly doesn't have to be expensive: stone, clay, bricks and time don't cost much. They're all part of the DIY-ness of fire cookery.

How you go about cooking with fire is completely down to you and what level you want to take it to. I never thought I would spend 22 hours cooking a whole cow in the centre of Dublin, but it was one of the best food experiences I have ever had and one that I learnt a lot from. So go forth and experiment, build things and cook on them. We don't cook over fire just for ourselves. Above all else, fire has a wonderful ability to bring us all together to share, celebrate and enjoy the food that is cooked over it, whether we are sitting around a hole in the garden or in the forest with a spitroast of venison.

# MAKING A FIRE

I'm a firm believer that if you are going to cook over fire, you should know how to make it from scratch. We're not talking matches and firelighters here, more about really getting back to basics: fire by friction, firesteels, tinder and wood selection. Being able to understand the fundamentals behind fire lighting and how fire burns not only makes you better at cooking with fire, but helps you get to grips with managing it over a sustained period.

As with most recipes, fire has its vital ingredients, of which there are three: fuel, oxygen and heat. In order to work efficiently there must be a combination of all three to enable air to pass through the fire and transfer the heat from one piece of fuel to the next. If your fire is too loaded with fuel, then you will restrict airflow. If your fuel is too sparse, then the heat transfer will burn out. There are lots of factors to consider, and while we certainly aren't a bushcraft or survival school, we only cook with fire and the aim is to teach people those skills, which is why fire workshops are a prominent feature of almost every course we offer.

When it comes to making a fire and cooking over it, one of the main considerations is fuel. Being in the middle of the woods, we're not short of it. The deciduous woodland we are based in has four prominent tree species that fire our

kitchen: birch, hornbeam, oak and ash. All of them burn slightly differently, have certain uses and even their own flavour profiles. They also come in a variety of different sizes, from the smallest twig to a hefty section of tree, so to get from setting fire to A to cooking over B there are quite a few steps in between. This is why if you work in the kitchen at HGC, a good solid axe is a very necessary part of your knife roll.

When we light our fires each day at the Treehouse, the first job is to split these logs down further with an axe in order to start with small bits of kindling to get the fire going and then gradually work up to the point where we can load whole logs on to heat the plancha (griddle) in the kitchen. When they burn down to coals we transfer them across to sit under the grill plate for grilling. We do also use charcoal, mainly for its efficiency in being ready to cook over a lot quicker as well as the different flavours they are available in.

All the fuel that fires the kitchen is cut from the wood we're based in. The wood is often seasoned in the round for up to two years before being split down into logs and left for a further six months. By the time we get a log drop at the Treehouse it's got a moisture content of below 20 per cent, perfectly seasoned and ready for a good burn.

Knowing how to make fire from scratch gives you the ability to cook virtually anywhere. To be able to look at the landscape around you and recognize which fuel is available and other natural materials to help you achieve this is a wonderful freedom that breaks us away from the conventional kitchen and back to how we always used to cook. The woods are not just for fuel: there are skewers, spits, asador crosses, grills and all shapes and sizes of pokers, tongs and pot hangers. The woods are not just a great place to cook; they're quite a useful workshop, too.

# FUEL SELECTION: flavours & uses

There are two distinct types of fuel you're likely to use when it comes to cooking over fire: wood or charcoal. We mostly use wood at HGC, but both work slightly differently and have their uses, depending on what you're cooking on and what it is you are planning to cook. For open fire pits, raised or on the ground, wood is preferable, as you have plenty of space to be able to have a 'feeder' fire constantly burning to produce coals you can then sweep across to one side to grill over. For kettle-style barbecues with lids, charcoal is preferable, as you are restricted on space and may not wish to spend the time burning down logs to grill on.

Although charcoal is a very efficient fuel source, wood provides more smoke and therefore more of an intense smoky flavour to whatever you're cooking. I like to have plenty of both regardless – always keep your options open. For getting a grill up to speed quickly, charcoal is perfect. Place it in a chimney starter and light with a roll of newspaper underneath. Provided it is good-quality charcoal, you can be ready to cook in about 20 minutes. With wood, you can double that time and maybe add a bit more.

When it comes to choosing wood to cook with and what's best to use, always go for what is most locally available to you. This might not seem easy if you live in a town or city, but there are plenty of online suppliers that can deliver to your doorstep. Only ever use deciduous hardwoods for cooking on, never coniferous softwoods. The wood we use is grown, cut and seasoned locally and provides us with a wonderful mix of useful fuel for our kitchen.

The following quartet of hardwood is hard to beat, so track them down if you can. Just remember: the golden rule with wood is to never grill anything over an open flame as it will taint the food with a black, acrid soot that will be very unpleasant.

## Silver birch
### Betula pendula

One of the best to get a fire started. The bark contains a lot of natural oils so it makes excellent tinder (see page 19). Small twigs make for a great primary fuel and burn fast, as do larger ones for a secondary fuel. It splits easily, burns bright and is the ideal wood for a campfire as it kicks out plenty of light. Great to cook on once it's burnt down to coals, but make sure all bark is burnt up before any cooking commences because it lets off a heavy black soot. Flavour is slightly sweet with faint aromatics.

## Hornbeam
### Carpinus betulus

This is a proper slow burner. A truly 'hard' wood, it's actually related to the birch but looks more like beech. This is the ultimate wood for good solid embers – it burns very hot and very slow. A favourite for the clay oven and the underground oven, it isn't easy to split as it does spalt, so the axe ends up chipping bits off rather than giving a solid split. Smoke is quite punchy but faintly sweet.

## Oak
### Quercus robur

Another ultimate slow burner that produces amazing fierce embers. Really good for grilling over and a great one for asadors and whole animal cookery. Not so easy to split, but the kindling from oak will give a solid heart to your fire once it's going. The smoke is quite a heavy one, but is distinctive, with hints of spice and a depth of smokiness.

## Ash
### Fraxinus excelsior

Ash has always been seen as useful due to its low moisture content, to the point that it will burn when it's 'green', as in freshly cut. Due to its structure, it splits very well and doesn't actually produce that much smoke when seasoned. Burns reasonably fast and has a fairly mild flavour with hints of sweetness.

### OTHER WOODS TO USE

Some alternative woods that are worthy of a mention, as we do use them depending on where we are cooking and what's available, include: beech, hazel, hawthorn and elm. And of course there are the fruitwoods, apple, plum and cherry, which add an amazing fruity sweetness to proceedings.

# FUEL SIZE & GRADING

When you go for back-to-basics fire lighting, preparation is key. Having all your fuel graded and ready to use is tremendously important. That way, once you ignite your tinder, you're in a good place to be able to gently feed the fire and watch it grow. This is the build-up before creating the spark that will ignite your birch bark or cramp ball fungus (see pages 20–21).

When looking for your primary sources of fuel, NEVER look on the ground. The ground holds a certain amount of residual moisture, which will make getting the fire going that much harder. Also, never use any freshly cut or 'green' wood, as it won't burn. Always look up to see what's hanging off other branches: these hanging twigs will be dead, air-dried and with little or no surface area to catch any past rainfall. That's what you want.

For other fuel grades, look for dead, dry standing wood, or dead limbs on trees. If it has a solid crack when snapped, it will be a good indication of dryness.

## FUEL GRADING COMES DOWN TO FOUR MAIN COMPONENTS:

## Tinder

Birch bark is one of the best tinders found in the woods. Essentially, it is a natural fire lighter due to its high oil content. When harvesting birch bark, just strip the fine peelings off live trees by hand. Honeysuckle bark, Old man's beard (*Clematis vitalba*), dead bracken, dry grasses and cotton wool are all good contenders, too.

## Primary fuel

Birch twigs. These also have natural oil present and will go up very quickly if gently fed onto the fire. You can make a bunched nest and carefully place it over the lit tinder and leave it to grow gradually.

## Secondary fuel

Once the primary tinder is going, gently start placing slightly larger twigs on, such as birch, hazel or hornbeam. Again, give the fire a chance to grow and don't blow on it unless all the flames have completely disappeared.

## Tertiary fuel

This is the final step before you can move on to split kindling and small logs. These should be roughly 2.5cm (1in) in diameter and carefully added to ensure plenty of airflow. By now, the fire should be quite well established. Birch, ash, hornbeam, hazel and oak are all good contenders at this stage.

# IGNITION

Both of the following techniques are designed to work with the Afterburner method (see page 23). Once you have all your fuel ready, before attempting to light using either technique, you must first prepare the ground. Start by clearing the ground of any dead leaves and twigs so you have a patch of bare earth, then lay down some of the tertiary fuel as a platform to light your fire on. This will protect the tinder from the damp ground and form a solid heart to the fire once burning. It helps to place a small log or larger stick at the back to rest your primary fuel on so it sits at a slight angle to allow for plenty of airflow.

## Firesteel and birch bark ignition

Using a firesteel is the main way we teach everyone to light fires down at HGC. Lighters and blowtorches are all very well, but a firesteel will rarely let you down once you have become proficient with it.

Firesteels are made up of a ferrocerium rod and a striker. They work even when wet and can last for up to 3,000 strikes. The bright sparks that fire out can ignite a huge range of tinders. You can also get purpose-made knives that work specifically with firesteels.

1 Take a small handful of birch bark, rub it between your hands to fluff it up a bit (this is called 'buffing'), then place it on your platform. When using the firesteel, you want to gently push the steel into the centre of the birch and place the striker on the steel. Keep the striker hand rigid and still and pull away with the steel so all the sparks are directed into the centre of the birch bark.

2 After a few strikes, a spark will land in the right place and the birch will catch light.

3 Once your birch bark is alight, carefully place on your primary fuel of small twigs and give the fire a chance to take hold, grow and burn well before adding more.

# Cramp ball fungus and dry grass

**1** Cramp ball fungus or King Alfred's cake (*Daldinia concentrica*) is a round black fungus found on dead ash trees. When growing, they are slightly brown and quite heavy as they're full of moisture. When dead and dry, they're similar to a piece of charcoal in look and weight.

**2** Before lighting make sure you have a tinder bundle of dry grass or straw ready and buff it between your hands to break up the fibres and fluff it up. Arrange your tinder bundle so it roughly resembles a bird's nest with a slight depression to place the cramp ball in once lit. Break the cramp ball fungus in half and place it on the floor. Using the firesteel, begin showering sparks directly onto the inside of the cramp ball. With a good strike, a spark will catch on the fungus and you will see it glow.

**3** At this point, pick it up and blow on it to make the ember grow. Once well established, hold the other half of the cramp ball against it and continue to blow to get that one burning – this will be your plan B in case the first one burns out.

**4** Place the smouldering cramp ball into the tinder bundle, hold the bundle between both hands and press together gently. Ensure the bundle is downwind from you before you blow on it. Start by blowing gently and then build up towards the end of your breath. Move the bundle away from you, inhale and then repeat. Make sure you have good contact with the tinder and the ember. Eventually a thick yellow smoke will start to emerge, which means it is about to burst into flames. Once it does, place it on your platform and carefully place on your primary fuel.

# AFTERBURNER

The Afterburner is a great way of building a cooking fire quickly, and is designed to build a solid core for your fire to grow around. It's loosely based on an A-frame that rises up from the floor in an arc to an angle of about 45 degrees that the flames, once established, really tear through. This technique is aimed at using wood that's in the round (pieces that haven't been cut or split) and by the time it reaches the point where it collapses in on itself, thanks to the A-frame structure, you will be getting close to a good bed of embers to grill over.

## Construction

**1** Following on from ignition (see page 20), which can be done with either cramp ball or birch bark, the primary fuel goes on first. Allow this a bit of time to grow and then lay down two larger sticks to form the first of the A-frames. Then lay down a few lengths of secondary fuel – birch is always the best.

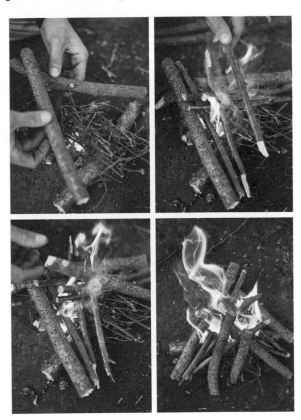

**2** As you build up your arc, always use slightly larger sticks on the outside and smaller ones on the inside: this helps the fire to collapse in on itself. If the flame is struggling to grow, don't add anything larger. Feed it a little more primary fuel and give it a bit of time. Only blow on a growing fire if the flame has completely disappeared, otherwise you're more likely to blow the fire out.

**3** Once it's well established, you can add larger bits of fuel and then start moving on to small logs cut down to size with an axe. This is very much a backwoods method of fire lighting ('backwoods' basically means 'out in the woods', so it's more natural and stripped back). It's a really efficient method for when you're out in the wild and unlikely to have a stack of logs to hand to start splitting down.

*TIP*

*If you have thicker lengths of dead, dry standing wood to cut down to size and don't have a folding saw, you can lever a length of wood between two offset trees and pull back until it breaks. You can even dictate the size you want by how much you pass between the trees.*

# THE HASHTAG:
## the mother of all fires

While the Afterburner method (see page 23) is a wonderfully indulgent way of backwoods fire lighting from scratch, the Hashtag, in contrast, is a very user-friendly method of getting your fire going. This is certainly our 'good game is a quick game' method at HGC. Essentially the mother of all our fires, it's what gets our kettles singing in the morning and lays the foundation for all the cooking we will be doing that day. We use it to light the clay oven and the smoker and transfer embers from it for any other fire we may need to set.

### FLAMERS

For ignition we use flamers, a firelighter made from renewable, untreated wood shavings that have been dipped in a refined paraffin wax. One or two are more than sufficient to get you fired up.

This technique will form an amazing base layer if you are cooking on wood alone, and an even better one if you are adding charcoal into the mix. Similar to the Afterburner, the Hashtag is designed to collapse when you hit your charcoal point. You can then either add more wood, if you need flame for pots and pans to cook over, or let it settle for grilling. You can even pile a batch of charcoal on the top prior to ignition if you are looking for a good bed of embers.

Once you start using this technique for getting your cooking fire going, you'll never look back. You may get someone trying to push you towards a wigwam setup, which is fine if you want to sit around a campfire and have a good source of light, but not really suitable for cooking on.

# Construction

**1** Using an axe or small hatchet, split down a load of logs into strips that are about 20–25cm (8–10in) long and 2.5cm (1in) thick. Birch and ash get going quickly, so are best for this, along with a couple of nice oak chunks as a hearty base. Keep a few slightly bigger pieces for your outer logs. The thinner ones should be placed as the inner Hashtag.

**2** Start building your stack by placing two larger oak splittings parallel to each other as the base, then lay four splittings across the top – the ones in the middle should be the thinnest to ensure a good burn. The more even and level, the better it will be.

**3** Continue to build the Hashtag up so it is about five layers deep, including the base. You can go higher, if needed – just make sure it doesn't turn into a game of Jenga. You can add a few handfuls of charcoal at this point, as well. Light a couple of firelighters, slip them in between the two base logs and simply leave well alone. If you want to pan-fry or boil a kettle, you should have flames roaring through the Hashtag in about 5–10 minutes.

# ASADOR

The world has been cooking whole animals on sticks for a very long time and using an asador or cooking 'a la cruz' (on the cross) is definitely one of life's great pleasures. The Argentinians are leaders in this form of cookery, which is a feast for the eyes as much as it is a way to yield sublime results from your meat.

You can purchase ready-made steel crosses online, but when you work in the woods, freshly cut lengths of hazel or birch are the preferred building materials. You can use wire to connect your frames and to fix the beast (here, a lamb) onto the frame, but jubilee clips (hose clamps) will make the job even easier.

## Equipment

1 x 1.8m/6ft length of hazel or birch for the main upright (5cm/2in diameter)
2 x 0.9m/3ft lengths of hazel or birch for the crossbeams (2.5cm/1in diameter)
2 x 1.8m/6ft lengths of hazel or birch (with Y-shaped ends for support sticks, if needed)
8 jubilee clips or 2mm/1⁄16in-diameter wire
screwdriver or drill, if using jubilee clips
pliers, if using wire

---

### BRINE RECIPE FOR DEER

You can cook a whole deer on the asador. It takes 4 hours and will require regular basting with a good-quality rendered fat in addition to our brine. To make the brine, simply combine all of the following ingredients and 480ml/16fl oz/2 cups water in a large bowl:

200g/7oz/1 cup coarse sea salt
240ml/8fl oz/1 cup red wine vinegar
240ml/8fl oz/1 cup olive oil
4–5 heads of garlic, peeled and finely chopped
50g/1¾oz/½ cup chilli flakes
25g/1oz/½ cup dried oregano
1 bunch of ground ivy leaves, finely chopped

---

## Construction

**1** First, get your fire on the go. A whole animal, such as a lamb or a deer, will be cooking for 4–5 hours, so you will need a good amount of wood to feed the fire. Wind direction is a key consideration that will ultimately control where your heat and smoke is going. Check the wind direction and make sure to set up your cross downwind so all the heat and smoke hits your whole animal.

**2** Lay the animal out on a table and, using the lengths of freshly cut wood, measure out a cross by laying the length for the main upright down the centre of the animal and the crossbeam lengths across the animal's front and back legs. Use the jubilee clips to put the frame together. Use two clips to fasten each of the cross beams onto the main upright in a criss-cross fashion so they are nice and tight. Set the cross aside while you work on the next step.

**3** Open up the animal, using a saw to open up the upper section through the spine. Flatten the animal out so that it has two surfaces to cook, then use the remaining jubilee clips to fasten all the legs to the frame and use wire to fasten the midriff and neck to the frame.

**4** Mix together your brine (or 'salmuera', as it's called in Argentina), which you will use to baste the meat as it cooks. The brine gradually builds up layers of seasoning on the lamb, so you'll be basting every 20 minutes.

**5** Dig one end of the frame into the ground and, if necessary (depending on the size of the animal you are using), use the support sticks to help hold it up. The support sticks will also allow you to spin the frame around with ease.

The most enjoyable part of this style of cookery is the management of it. Your optimum heat control is glorious in its simplicity and the 10-second rule applies here: hold your hand just in front of the animal and if your hand feels like it's on fire by the time you count to 10, you're good to go. Start cooking with the inside, or rib side, of the animal facing the fire. You will need to turn the asador several times during cooking, but once you get a feel for the fire, the rest will flow.

# HOW TO BUILD A SIMPLE CLAY OVEN

If there is a missing piece of the puzzle when it comes to outdoor cookery, then the clay oven is it. While we can achieve a lot with so many methods such as baking in embers or ash, using Dutch ovens and underground ovens, none of these methods really give you the ability to properly check and see how your food is doing. The clay oven gives us the freedom to do so with relative ease and opens up another level of cooking with fire. It is extremely versatile and can be used for baking, roasting whole pheasants or cuts of meat, cooking vegetables, pizzas, smoking whole bulbs of garlic and even keeping food warm. One thing I love to see when the clay oven is roaring is the 'dragon's lick' of flame dancing across the roof of the oven.

It may seem like a bit of a challenge, but the materials used and the construction of a clay oven is actually very basic. In terms of materials all you need are bricks, sand, water, clay and straw.

While most clay ovens have a brick arch at the front, it is entirely possible to build one without. The majority of clay ovens I have built haven't had one, which simplifies the entire construction process. The instructions below are based on the original clay oven we had at HGC and the photos are of said oven coming together.

## Raw materials and equipment needed

You will need a fair amount of material – this will be dictated by the surface area of your plinth: a good size is roughly 1.5m² (16 ft²). For the mix for the actual oven you will need 2 parts sand to 1 part clay and a bit of straw to mix in to help bind the mix together during construction. You will also need some extra sand to make the former that you will build the oven around.

Bricks, sand and clay can all be purchased at your nearest builders' merchants, but if you live in an area that is clay based, you can source that naturally – look especially for areas near water.

### SITING YOUR CLAY OVEN

Before you start building your oven, you want to choose a good spot for it. Undercover is ideal, if possible. I would recommend building some sort of plinth for it to sit on that's about 1m (3ft) in height. This can be made of wood, stone or bricks, which can be put together with mud and clay and back filled with earth or rubble. The top of your plinth should be levelled off with sand and have a layer of bricks on top, which will eventually be the floor of the oven.

# Construction

**1** The first stage is to build a sand former on top of the bricks, which will eventually be the inside dimension of your oven. This acts as a mould around which to build and support the insulating layers of clay/sand mix that will go on it. The height of the former should be around 35cm (14in) and you should aim to leave at least 25cm (10in) between the edge of the former and the edge of your plinth, as the walls of the oven will be up to 18cm (7in) thick by the time the oven is finished.

**2** Once you have built the former the next stage is to cover it with a few layers of wet newspaper. The main reason for doing this is that when the oven is complete and you are ready to open it up and remove the sand former, the newspaper will have kept the sand separated from the clay. This will enable you to tell which is the former and which is the clay when you hollow it out. It will also burn away when you fire it up for the first time.

**3** To make your mix you need to have a ratio of 2 parts sand to 1 part clay. Use a wheelbarrow for mixing and a bucket to measure out the clay and sand. In between adding in the buckets, chuck in a few handfuls of straw and distribute evenly to help bind the materials. When the wheelbarrow is quite full, add a little bit of water then start to mix everything together using a spade. You want a consistency that is still quite firm, moist and able to mould well without cracking. Add a little more water if needed.

**4** To start building the first layer of the clay oven, take a good handful of the mix and shape it into a rough brick, place it on the plinth up against the former and pat it in gently. The first layer should be roughly 10cm (4in) thick. Continue making roughly shaped bricks and work around the oven until they join and the base layer is finished. Ensure that each brick put down adheres well to the other. Repeat this process and continue to work all the way up to the top of the former till it is completely covered. Wet your hands and smooth the entire layer down by hand then leave to dry out for at least 3 hours.

**5** To make the chimney, take a sharpened stick roughly 5cm (2in) in diameter and drive it in through the clay and into the former at a 45-degree angle on the front side of the oven. Wet your hands and smooth the entire layer down by hand then leave to dry out for at least 24 hours.

The next stage is to add the final insulating layer using the exact same process as in step 4, only this time the layer should be about 8cm (3in) thick and can extend all the way to the edge of the plinth.

**6** Once the final layer is on, remove the stick that you put in for your chimney hole and then it's time to remove the sand former. Start by marking out the size of the clay oven entrance and ensure it's big enough to fit in oven trays and pizza peels.

**7** Using a machete or chef's knife slice into the clay/sand mix, which should still be a slightly bit moist. Cut around the line you have marked for your entrance until you feel you have hit the sand former and gradually remove the clay/sand mix from where the oven entrance will be. Once you see newspaper you will have got through the two layers and reached the sand former.

**8** Remove all of the sand until the clay oven is empty. Finish off the entrance to the oven by rounding off the edges with wet hands.

At this stage it's best to leave the clay oven to dry for a further 24 hours, although you can light a very small fire with a bit of kindling in the centre of the oven to help the drying process.

As the oven dries and you start to use it, you will need to use a pure clay slip, just made of clay mixed with a bit of water, to fill in the cracks. The cracks are absolutely fine, as it shows that the oven is working well — it will expand and contract. The first proper firing should take place a few days after being finished. Build a small fire in the mouth of the oven and gradually ease it in and keep adding fuel. Once your oven is firing at about 400°C (752°F) then it is ready to cook on. Laser temperature guns are the best tool for measuring the heat. Push all the wood to the back of the oven and try to keep a flame going, as that will help keep the temperature up.

TIP

*It's best to cover your clay oven when not in use, as rain will not be that helpful for its longevity.*

# SWEDISH LOG CANDLE

Swedish log candles are truly natural stoves that provide a useful cooking surface to begin with and then, as they burn, become your grill. They are far more popular in continental Europe than in the UK, but I would urge you to give one a go. Even if you aren't going to cook over it, they are awesome to stand around for warmth and light, and they also look impressive.

A self-feeding, one-piece fire unit, the Swedish log candle is an ingenious concept that's incredibly simple to make. You'll need a tape measure and a chainsaw (please make sure you are trained in using a chainsaw and wear the necessary protective gear for operating one). Alternatively, you can, if your muscles are feeling up to it, use a handsaw. However, this will make lighting the Swedish log candle a lot harder because the handsaw's narrower blade will make a smaller gap than a chainsaw's wider blade, so less air will be able to flow through.

Because of the way it burns, the Swedish log candle can provide four practical uses. To begin with, you get an excellent light source. After half an hour of burning (or even less), the flat, circular top is ideally suited to put a kettle or skillet on. After an hour, the log candle starts churning out a fair bit of heat, and when you get into the second hour of burning, it'll be hot enough for you to drop down a chunky kebab and slow-roast it on all sides.

## WHICH WOOD TO USE

Base your choice on the main function you're wanting your log candle to provide. If you want to cook over it, choose a hardwood such as beech, oak, apple, hornbeam or cherry. Avoid softwoods for cooking because they will taint the meat and cover pots and pans in soot. However, they are great if you are just looking for warmth and light. Whatever you use, make sure it is well-seasoned. Well-seasoned wood is wood that has been cut fresh, stacked and allowed to dry out for about two years.

## Construction

**1** Select your log. The standard dimensions that we use are 60cm (24in) long with a diameter of 25cm (10in). Don't let dimensions get in your way, though. There is no reason you couldn't use a tree trunk that's 1.8m (6ft) long with a 1.25m (4ft) diameter and cook a whole animal in it. Go big or go home.

**2** Ensure that both ends have level surfaces. The thickest end will be the base.

**3** Set your log upright on the ground and, using a pencil and measuring tape, mark the top with guidelines for where you are going to cut. What you are aiming to create will look like the top of a pie that has been cut into six pieces.

**4** Using a chainsaw, make the first cut straight across the middle of the log and rip the chainsaw downwards at a steady pace until you get to 15cm (6in) from the bottom. At this point, tip the chainsaw down and inwards to make the cut lower on the outside and about 3mm (⅛in) deep. This will help draw more air up the log once it is lit, ensuring a better burn. Be careful not to cut all the way through.

**5** Repeat the cuts on the other marked lines down to the 15cm (6in) mark and remember to tip the chainsaw inwards when you get to the base for airflow.

**6** To light the log candle, stuff wood shavings, birch bark, broken-up natural firelighters or any other kind of tinder into all the cuts and ignite with a blowtorch or lighter. It might take a bit of time to get the log candle burning, but once it's going, there's no stopping it. The burn time for one of our stand-sized logs, like the one pictured, can be up to 3 hours.

# DIRTY COOKING

If you think that a sausage rolling off the grill and into the coals is a loss, lose that fear right now because that sausage will taste better than all the others. 'Dirty' cooking is the purest form of fire cookery there is. Also known as 'clinching' (perhaps because it sounds cleaner), dirty cooking means cooking food directly on hot coals, just as our ancestors would have done. It's a safe bet, too, that early man didn't have a stainless steel grill to cook on.

Fire cookery was a key factor in the evolution of mankind: it changed us forever. Meat is high-calorie stuff in a condensed package. In comparison, fruits, vegetable matter and berries don't contain nearly the same levels of calories. That means early humans spent a lot of time and energy grazing, gathering in high volume and digesting such foods. When early man first paired meat with fire, good things happened. Cooking meat made it even more digestible, allowing more energy to be diverted elsewhere: to our brains. This led to a series of developments: jawlines changed, as we no longer had to spend so much time 'chewing the cud'; teeth changed to deal with meat better; and, above all, man began to create things, such as tools, clothing and language. And here we are.

Just like charcoal, when wood burns, it gradually breaks down and becomes the embers you're going to grill over. For fire, oxygen is essential to the equation. When you drop a slab of meat directly onto hot coals, there is no space for the oxygen to get in, so the heat is transferred directly into the meat from the wood or charcoal, without any flame (though you may get the occasional flare-up, especially if there's fat content on your meat). The flavour is much more intense than anything that's been on a grill, and dirty cooking is actually a lot gentler than you would think. The 'char' effect on both meat and vegetables adds to the end product, giving a depth of flavour that grilling won't deliver. The Maillard reaction is in play here, too: heat breaks down proteins in the meat into amino acids, which then react with the sugars in the meat to create that wonderful, flavour-packed crust. Dirty cooking is this on steroids.

## DIRTY COOKING TIPS

About forty per cent of the food we cook at HGC is done directly on hot coals. Here are a few pointers to help you on your path to cooking like we did back in 10,000 BCE:

Make sure you are using proper charcoal, such as lumpwood (hardwood lump charcoal) or coals from natural wood. No unsustainable rainforest product or compressed blocks of inferior charcoal.

If you're burning your wood down for embers, good woods to use are oak, beech, ash, hornbeam, birch and chestnut.

Before you put any meat or fish on the coals, be sure to give the coals a good fanning with a tray, or something similar, to get rid of any ash.

Make sure you have a really good bed of embers ready. It should be at least 5cm (2in) thick, with a good spread so that when you go for a flip you are able to put the meat on a fresh bed of coals because the place where it was cooking will have lost most of its heat and energy.

If cooking on burnt-down logs, make sure you have a second one up to speed and ready to go, so you can flip the one just used back onto the fire in case you need it again.

Don't forget your veggies. Veg such as onions, leeks, peppers, tomatoes, chillies and beetroot (beets) tend to form a crust or charring on the skin that can be removed or brushed off. But make sure you leave some on there for flavour because the carbon is clean and wonderful.

# THE SMOKE TIPI

Preserving meat is as old as the hills, and this method of smoke-drying really takes us back to our origins. Back when our hunter-gatherer ancestors were slaying wild beasts twice the size of the animals we hunt today, they would have a huge glut of meat and no fridge or freezer to put it in for long-term storage. Of course, Mother Nature gave them all the tools they needed to solve that problem, and we continue the tradition today.

The ideal time for smoke-drying is in spring or summer when there are plenty of leaves on the trees to provide the coverage you will need to go around the tipi. Some recipes can take up to 15 hours to complete, so it's perfect for a long day or weekend out in the woods, when you have the time to keep an eye on it. You can reduce the smoke-drying time by cutting thinner strips of meat, but do be aware that the meat will shrink by up to fifty per cent as it dries. You can also smoke your meat outside for as long as you have time and then finish the process at home in a dehydrator or oven, but this little project is a brilliant excuse to camp out in the woods.

# Construction

**1** Cut down three lengths of hazel or birch, each around 2.25m (7ft) long, and another three lengths that are each around 75cm (30in) long for the rack. Sycamore and sweet chestnut are also good sources of straight lengths. Try to get as many of these lengths as possible from a single tree or sapling to limit your impact on the wild. Take the three 2.25m (7ft) lengths and stand them up and form a tripod, joining and tying them together at the 1.8m (6ft) mark with wire, string or twine. Next tie the three smaller lengths onto the tripod at about 20cm (8in) off the ground to create the rack on which your skewered meat will rest.

**2** Cut down plenty of green leafy boughs or lower branches that spread out like fronds. Hazel, birch, hornbeam and beech are good sources. These will serve as a screen to keep the smoke in and the wind out. You'll want to keep one side of the tipi open to tend to the fire, so check for wind direction and then tie these branches around the sides, and especially the bottom, of the tipi so that they block the wind and hit the back of the tipi. If these branches are long enough, you can hook them into the top of the tipi.

**3** Get a small fire going and place some large oak logs next to it so they start to burn and smoulder. Let the logs burn down so that you have a nice gentle heat and lots of smoke, but no flames. Keep a jug of water next to the fire to extinguish any minor flare-ups. Using any offcuts from the hazel, whittle down a bunch of skewers and thread your meat onto the skewers (see page 107), leaving a 2cm (¾in) gap between each piece. Mount them on the rack and let the smoke tipi get to work. Have a few more logs ready to add when needed and keep an eye out for any flare-ups.

# THE UNDERGROUND OVEN

I first learned this technique in Fiji, when some farmers in the village we were staying in offered to cook a whole pig for us. The underground oven is an ingenious, yet simple, culinary invention that enables you to cook a lot of food with nothing more than what nature provides: wood, earth, vegetation and stone. These days, we do use a few extra bits and pieces to make everything easier, but the basic principle of 'steam-roasting' remains the same.

Many cultures around the world have different variations of the underground oven. In New Zealand it is referred to as a 'hangi' and across the South Pacific it is widely known as an 'umu'. The Pacific has a rich tradition of cooking underground and passing down tips as well as the stones themselves from generation to generation. Earth ovens in Europe appear in the archaeological record during the Neolithic period, becoming more prominent in the Bronze and Iron Ages.

## Raw materials and equipment needed

Have all of your materials on hand before you start. Determine the weight of whatever you intend to cook. You'll need roughly a third more that weight in basalt rocks, or in a similar igneous rock that won't fracture or explode under heat. Do not use flint. A good place to find suitable rocks is along old, disused railway tracks. You might also be able to buy them online or from a construction materials supplier.

For wood, you will need enough logs to fill the underground oven once it's burning, including a pile of small kindling, some medium-sized wood and a pile of larger hardwood logs, such as oak, beech or hornbeam.

To cover the oven, you'll need a section of corrugated iron for the lid. This should be a little bigger than the 60cm (2ft) square pit and should be available from a construction materials supplier. You will also need large burdock leaves to help seal the edges of the oven. A few fresh, straight lengths of hazel or sweet chestnut, cut to fit on top of the hot stones, will help to keep the meat from having direct contact with the stones.

You'll also need a tool for moving the hot rocks (such as a spade or a shovel) and a tray or similar tool for fanning the fire.

# Construction

**1** Dig a pit that's 60cm (2ft) wide by 60cm (2ft) long and 45cm (18in) deep. When digging, pile up the soil beside the pit for covering the oven later.

**2** Build a small fire in the bottom of the pit using the Hashtag technique (see page 24) and gradually build it up, going from smallest to largest in fuel size until the pit is full. Once the fire is raging, start piling the rocks in the middle on top of the wood. You now have to wait till the fire has burnt down and sunk into the pit with the weight of the rocks, which will slowly heat up to cooking temperature. This can take 45 minutes to an hour. It's worth fanning the fire with a tray every so often to work some oxygen into it.

**3** While the fire is getting ready, prepare your meat. Front and back haunches are ideal for this type of cooking, and deboning them will reduce their cooking time. A whole chicken or duck will take 1½ hours; for larger joints allow 3–4 hours. This is a primitive cooking method, so you won't be able to check the meat to see if it's done. Underground ovens are not an exact science, so only experience will help you perfect the process.

Season the meat well, add some herbs or the rub of your choice and then wrap the meat well in burdock leaves or foil, which will help retain moisture and keep the juices in. Alternatively, you can use a metal baking tray and cover it with foil.

**4** To see if the oven is ready, check the heat of the stones by flicking some water over the rocks. If it evaporates immediately, you are good to go. Use a spade or shovel to flatten out the stones.

**5** Place the cut hazel lengths over the stones and put the wrapped bundle of meat or the metal baking tray on top. Cover with the corrugated iron lid, then arrange the burdock leaves around the edges. Pile the soil from digging the pit over the top until you cannot see even the slightest wisp of smoke emerging from around the edges and the lid has a good layer of soil on top of it to act as insulation. You should use all the soil you originally dug out. Lay a shovel or an 'X' of sticks over the top so no one walks across it. Take a note of what time you sealed the oven and allow an extra half hour on top of how long you expect it to cook.

**6** When the meat is ready, scrape back the soil with your shovel, carefully remove the leaves from around the edges and remove the corrugated iron. Note: they'll be very hot! Remove the meat from the oven, using tongs, fire gloves or oven gloves, unwrap it and tuck in.

Your underground oven will stay hot for at least another 12 hours, so make full use of it. Anything that you want to give a good long slow cook is worth going in, just reseal it and let nature do its thing.

## UNDERGROUND OVEN TIPS

Always make sure you use igneous stones. Formed under a huge amount of heat, they have the capacity to hold heat. Bricks and steel will not do a good job.

Build a proper furnace before the rocks go on.

Keep a good eye on the rocks to determine when they have reached the right temperature. If they go beyond that, the fire will start to die out, the rocks will begin to lose heat and you will have to start again.

# THE SELF-FEEDING FIRE

The self-feeding fire produces a nice gentle heat that rises up, providing good indirect, ambient heat coverage to cook by. This type of fire is also useful for sleeping around, because there's no need for anyone to feed it during the night.

## Construction

**1** Hammer the two hazel poles into the ground at 45 degrees, spacing them far enough apart so that your logs can sit on them. If necessary, hammer in two supporting poles behind these in an 'X' shape.

**2** Position a log at the bottom and hammer in the wooden pegs at the base to support the bottom log, then stack your logs above the bottom log.

**3** Light a fire at the base and add a bit of charcoal to get things going. Then bang in the two Y-shaped poles for a spit to rest on. They should be positioned a little away from the fire so that the meat is cooked indirectly, by a wall of fire. You can always sweep a few coals underneath the spit if you need more heat when cooking.

## Equipment

2 x freshly cut straight poles of hazel or birch, about 1.5m/5ft long

hammer

2 x freshly cut straight poles of hazel or birch, about 1.5m/5ft long, as extra support, if needed

2 x freshly cut wooden pegs, at least 30cm/12in long

charcoal

2 x Y-shaped poles of freshly cut hazel or other hardwood, about 60cm/23½in long

*TIP*

*Only use freshly cut wood to build the frame of the self-feeding fire to ensure the frame doesn't burn.*

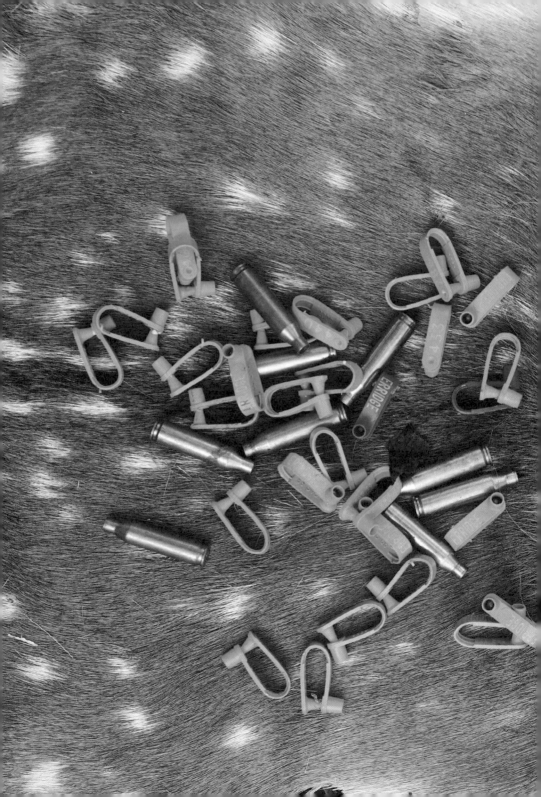

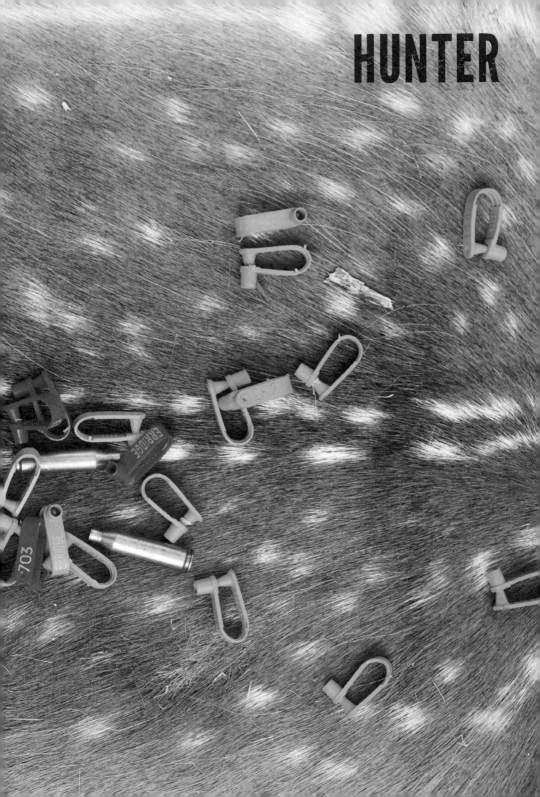

"The ethical side of
procuring your own
protein ticks a lot
of boxes: locally
sourced, low food
miles, free range..."

# DEER

Deer have always fascinated me. There is something slightly regal about them in the way they move and behave that suggests they are well above any of the other furred creatures that inhabit the same landscape. Ashdown Forest in Sussex is well known for its deer population, and growing up in this amazing part of the country it was rare not to come across them on a regular basis. My bedroom window looked down over the paddock, which was bordered by dense woodland. Most mornings there would be fallow deer pottering about, browsing on the brambles. They were always a pleasure to see; they are beautiful creatures to observe, majestic and perfectly designed by nature.

IT WASN'T UNTIL MANY YEARS LATER that I really got to know deer, up close and personal. When HGC began, I was familiar with venison, the collective term for deer, as a meat. I had eaten it and enjoyed it, but I had always worked with small game. This was something entirely different.

After a while, we began getting in whole deer carcasses and started meeting all sorts of people who showed us the different ways in which they broke them down. Not in the same way a butcher would — there were no saws, cleavers or blocks — everything was stripped off the carcass into primal cuts using nothing more than a small hunting knife. The quality of meat was incredible and the process had such a primitive feel to it that deer butchery quickly became something of a hobby and a regular part of our courses. After four years of becoming very proficient in breaking down whole carcasses, performing seam butchery on front and back haunches, and cooking them in all sorts of ways, I started to feel that I had no connection between the deer I would see in the wild to the one hanging on the butcher's hook. It was time to move on from popping bunnies and shooting pigeons and get stuck into deer.

Deer are largely responsible for our evolution. Being the predominant prey species across the planet, our ancestors got so much from them: meat for protein, bones and antlers for tools, and hides for clothing and bedding. That is why I have so much respect for this animal. The first time I shot a deer was 21 January 2015. It was a muntjac because I wanted to start with the smallest species and work my way up. Not a single piece of that deer went to waste, and as I write, there he is mounted on the wall. It's the only 'trophy' I have to remind me of where this journey began for me.

Deer stalking definitely connected the two. It was a hard one for me to begin with — I like to observe them and appreciate them, but then there is a responsibility in all of us as carnivores and a deeper connection to the meat we consume when it has been shot, gralloched (gutted) and butchered by your own hand. It can be said that hunting your own meat is the closest you, as a carnivore, can come to being an ethical vegetarian while being an omnivore. Many vegetarians share the same views as a lot of hunters on mass-produced meat and the processes involved. We all agree on the same things, but our approach to the issue is different. It is, I feel, easier for non-meat eaters to understand eating wild meat. The ethical side of procuring your own protein ticks a lot of boxes: locally sourced, low food miles, free range, wild, excellent meat quality and dispatched cleanly and efficiently. If you are an avid meat eater, then deer stalking is definitely a pastime I would recommend. The Resources section on page 170 has information on how to go about it.

# SPECIES GUIDE

At HGC we focus on only four of the deer species that are available to us locally: predominantly fallow and roe but also occasionally sika and muntjac. Of the six deer species we have in the UK only two are native: red deer and roe deer. All of them have slightly subtle differences in flavour, with red and roe deer being the strongest in terms of taste.

## Red deer
### Cervus elaphus
**SEASONS** Stags: 1 August–30 April (England, Wales and Northern Ireland); 1 July–20 October (Scotland).
Hinds: 1 November–31 March (England, Wales and Northern Ireland); 21 October–15 February (Scotland).
**NOTES** Native, largest of the herd species. Predominantly found in Scotland, scattered populations around the UK.
**FLAVOUR PROFILE** Strong venison flavour. Deep red in colour, rich and gamey.

## Sika deer
### Cervus nippon
**SEASONS** Stags: 1 August–30 April (England, Wales and Northern Ireland); 1 July–20 October (Scotland).
Hinds: 1 November–31 March (England, Wales and Northern Ireland); 21 October–15 February (Scotland).
**NOTES** Non-native, introduced in the 1860s from East Asia. Herd species. Found dotted all over the UK in parks and estates.
**FLAVOUR PROFILE** Very similar to fallow, not too strong and slightly sweeter in flavour. One of the best in terms of flavour, often comes with a good fat content.

## Fallow deer
### Dama dama
**SEASONS** Bucks: 1 August–30 April (England and Wales); 1 August–30 April (Scotland). Does: 1 November–31 March (England and Wales); 21 October–15 February (Scotland).
**NOTES** Non-native, introduced by the Normans for hunting and meat. Herd species, very common throughout the UK.
**FLAVOUR PROFILE** Fairly mild and definitely an entry-level variety. Lacks the strong gamey flavour of red deer. More like a cross between beef and lamb.

# Roe deer
## Capreolus capreolus
**SEASONS** Bucks: 1 April–31 October (England and Wales); 1 April–20 October (Scotland). Does: 1 November–31 March (England and Wales); 21 October–31 March (Scotland).
**NOTES** Native, territorial species found in small groups. Smaller and lighter framed deer, very common throughout the UK.
**FLAVOUR PROFILE** Similar to red deer, but not as strong. Slightly gamey, rich red meat, very good texture.

# Chinese water deer
## Hydropotes inermis
**SEASONS** Bucks and does: 1 November–31 March (England, Wales, Northern Ireland and Scotland).
**NOTES** Non-native; introduced to London Zoo in the 1800s. Male has no antlers, just large protruding tusks. Small, territorial species found in small groups. Found mostly north of London and East Anglia.
**FLAVOUR PROFILE** Fairly light coloured meat, similar to that of fallow deer in taste. Fairly mild, great texture.

# Muntjac
## Muntiacus reevesi
**SEASONS** No closed season on bucks or does and breeds all year round.
**NOTES** Non-native. Introduced in the 1890s to Woburn estate and spread like wildfire. The smallest of our deer, territorial and found in small numbers. Believed to be one of the oldest deer species in the world. Males have tusks and small antlers.
**FLAVOUR PROFILE** One of the most flavoursome of all the deer species. Slightly sweet, slightly gamey with an amazing texture – there's just not a lot of it as they are so small.

## AMERICAN SPECIES OF DEER
The above species of deer are found in the UK and various parts of Europe. In the USA, however, the following deer species are most common: Elk, Moose, Caribou, Mule Deer, white-tailed deer and black-tailed deer. Collectively they all fall under 'venison' but also have their own subtle differences when it comes to flavour profile.

# DEER BUTCHERY

The expression 'there's more than one way to skin a cat' certainly applies to deer butchery, and our approach has evolved a lot since HGC began back in 2011. Over the years, we've met some wonderful, knowledgeable folk from all over the country, who have generously shared their techniques for skinning and breaking down a deer carcass into primal cuts, which has helped shape and influence our own deer butchery process to become what it is today.

Ash, who is pictured in this whole butchery section, is one of the original HGC crew. We began our journey with deer at the same time and our passion for the butchery side of handling this incredible wild meat quickly led to sourcing it ourselves. What you'll find here is our way, the hunter's way, of breaking down a carcass. It applies to any deer species and other than a set of gambrels (stainless steel hooks) to hang the deer on, it doesn't involve the use of lots of butchery equipment. The first deer butchered at HGC was a roebuck, done with a set of flint tools the course attendees had knapped themselves. Like I said – things have evolved since then.

## Skinning

Most of the skinning process is done by hand with only minimal use of the knife to separate certain parts of the skin.

**1** Make a small pocket with your finger on the inner part of the haunch and then, using a knife or a gut opener, run it all the way up the inside leg. Be careful not to cut into the meat. Then, with a rolling wrist action, work the skin off both sides of the front haunch and up towards the top of the haunch and around the tendon, then cut through the skin, away from the meat, to release it.

**2** Grasping the pelt with both hands, use your body weight to pull down the skin with a steady, gradual motion. The key thing to look out for is where the tip of the flank starts. Once this appears, place your thumb against the tip of the flank and push the flank away from the skin. Draw the skin down over the tail so the tail is exposed and then cut through the disc between the bones of the tail to release the skin.

**3** With one hand pulling the skin from the carcass, lock your other arm and use

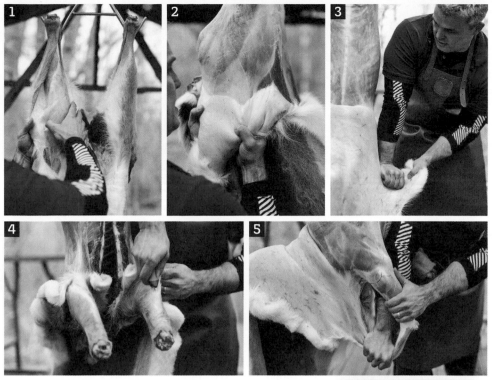

your body weight to ease the skin gradually down to the shoulders. This will reveal the 'tiger stripes', which, if still on the carcass and not the skin, shows you're doing a good job.

**4** Once you get to the shoulders, expose the 'elbow' of the front haunch and, using your knife or gut opener, run it down to the end of the front haunch.

**5** Work the skin off both sides of the front haunch until you can make a gap through the front side of the haunch

and then place your hand through the gap and grasp the skin firmly. With a strong downwards motion, force the skin off the end of the front haunch, then just keep working the skin down from the shoulders till you are past the neck and pull the skin off the end of the carcass.

**6** You should be left with a very clean pelt with minimal flesh on it, perfect for tanning.

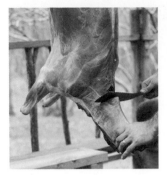

## Neck butchery

Start by removing the neck, using a machete, cleaver or axe. Pull down on the end the neck and slice down to the bone, then chop through the vertebrae and remove that section.

## Shoulders

**1** Take hold of the end of the shoulder on the shank and give it a wiggle so you can see where the shoulder blade is moving underneath the flank. Then, using the knife, make a cut into the carcass and slice down towards the elbow.

**2** Once you've made this cut to open up the shoulder, work the knife on the inside of the shoulder blade itself, from the bottom of the ribs and up towards the spine until you can remove the entire shoulder, which will only be connected with muscle and sinew.

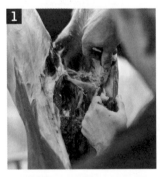

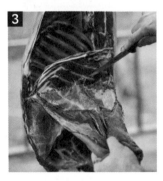

## Flanks

**1** To remove the flanks, start by cutting with the knife from where the flanks connect to the pelvis. Follow the flank around the edge of the back haunch until you work the knife up to the edge of the backstrap.

**2** Slide the blade down the top of the flank along the edge of the backstrap until you hit the ribcage, then score down over the ribs with the knife until you get to where you have removed the shoulder.

**3** Pull open the flank and make sweeping cuts across the ribcage, pulling the flank off as you go. This is similar to the way you would fillet a fish. Once the flanks are removed, you can either remove the intercostal muscles while the carcass is still hanging or do it after you have cut off the rib sections.

## Pencil fillets

**1** To remove the pencil fillets (or 'true' fillets), start by removing any suet that sits over the top of them. (Suet is the fat that sits around where the kidneys were.) Make a long sweeping cut from the top of the fillet down the inside edge where it is closest to the spine, then score around the outside edge, following the shape of the pencil fillet.

**2** Gradually part the fillets from the floating ribs, using your thumb and handling with care as the fillets are very tender. Work the knife up to the very top of the pencil fillet, where it disappears into the back haunch by the pelvis.

**3** Make a cut at the top of the fillet to release the end of it and then, running your knife down the inside edge of the fillet, carefully lift it out until it is completely free. Repeat with the other side.

## WHAT'S THE BEST KNIFE FOR DEER BUTCHERY?

We have used many different knives over the years for all types of game butchery. For deer butchery the key considerations are to have a blade that holds a good edge, is made from stainless steel, is fairly stiff to deal with more heavy-duty work and has a handle with a good grip. For finer work such as removing backstraps, a more flexible boning knife is preferable. This is my selection of knives I've used over the last six years, from custom-made hunting knives through to the standard Mora clipper knife on the left – this is the knife all our customers on courses use for their butchery. Find what works for you and bear in mind the cost of the knife doesn't always reflect in its performance.

## Backstraps

**1** Start by making a cut following the shape of the base of the haunch and slice through towards the spine.

**2** Once you have hit the spine, use the knife to gently score down the side of the spine, keeping the blade tight against the vertebrae as you cut down all the way to where you removed the neck. Repeat this gradual sweeping cut until you can hear the knife edge running along the ribs.

**3** Move over to working on the side of the backstrap that sits above the ribs. Start by making short, oscillating movements with the tip of the blade until you can open it up with your thumb and work to part it from the ribs right up against the spine.

**4** The final manoeuvre is to loosen the backstrap from the top just below the haunch and draw out the backstrap. Do this while making small cuts where it is still connected at the point where the ribs meet the spine until the entire backstrap is released. Repeat with the other side.

## Ribs and spine removal

**1** Once the backstraps have been removed, take your machete, cleaver or axe and use it to punch through the ribs to remove the ribcage, staying nice and tight against the spine until you have gone through all the ribs. Be sure to stand to one side while doing this and be careful when you get to the final one because they are quite easy to cut through. Repeat with the other side.

**2** Next, remove the spine. Start by cutting into the vertebrae on the intervertebral disc (the bit between the vertebrae). With a bit of gentle persuasion and working the knife, you will be able to make your way through it.

**3** Get hold of the back haunches and grip the spine. Pull it up until you hear it crack and separate then twist and pull to remove the spinal column.

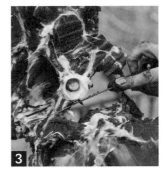

## Back haunches

**1** To remove the back haunches, start by making a cut at the base where you removed the tail and make a sweeping cut on one side of what remains of the spine. This will gradually release the rump while at the same time starting the separation of haunch and pelvis.

**2** Swing the haunches around and unclip the side you are working on off the gambrels so you can open the haunches out. Using the knife, slice in towards the pelvis, letting the weight of the haunch do most of the work for you.

**3** You will come up against the ball and socket, which has a thin layer of cartilage that connects both sides. The knife will work through this easily. Keep cutting in with the knife to cut the meat off the pelvis until one haunch is free and then repeat with the other side.

# Back haunches seam butchery

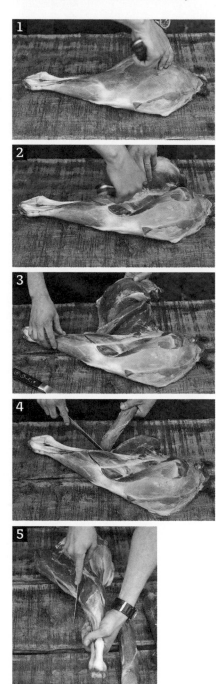

While you can cook an entire back haunch of venison as it is, you can make it go a lot further by breaking the haunch down into different cuts. Seam butchery separates the muscles in the leg into individual cuts, by following the white lines of sinew that hold them all together. In my opinion, two of the finest deer cuts, the fat flank and the bullet, sit inside the back haunch and it is for those two reasons that you would certainly want to break them down.

**1** When starting your seam butchery, always have the outside of the haunch facing up at you. The most obvious cut that will be directly in front of you is the silverside, which will be the first one to remove. It also, very conveniently, has the most obvious white line or 'seam' that you are going to want to hit first. Start by running your knife down this line to open up the haunch.

**2** The silverside is shaped like a slightly skewed rectangle. As you use your knife to separate the membrane, roll the silverside off with your other hand.

**3** With the silverside removed and the haunch opened up, you can now see the salmon fillet underneath and the fat flank under that, all still connected.

**4** Once you have removed the silverside, take off the salmon fillet in the same way. Be aware that it does nuzzle its tip on the underside of the haunch against the shank, so you might have to flip over the haunch to take off the last bit.

**5** Next, remove the shank from the haunch. Start by slicing in with the knife between the shank and the fat flank. You can also make a cut on the front side of the haunch in the 'knee' area to loosen the shank up a bit.

**6** Feel around for the femur. You will need to cut this out to remove the shank. Do this by working the knife up either side of the femur, cutting as close to the bone as you can until you can remove the whole shank. At this stage you will also want to take off the rump, which sits at the end of the femur.

**7** What you have left now are sometimes known as front round and back round, but these are actually three separate cuts and what we refer to as the 'scrag', which often ends up in the mincer. Start by removing the D-joint from the scrag and back round. This can mostly be done by hand – you just have to roll it off and separate the membrane that holds it to the others.

**8** Now onto the stars of the show: the fat flank (also known as pavé of venison) and the bullet. They are not as easy to separate as the other cuts because they don't have a particularly obvious line dividing them, so this is where feeling your way with your fingers really helps before charging in with a knife. Once you have found where they separate, bring in the knife.

**9** You will find that both bullet and fat flank are well attached to the scrag, so it's a case of rolling them off the scrag using a sweeping motion with your knife until they are both separated into individual cuts.

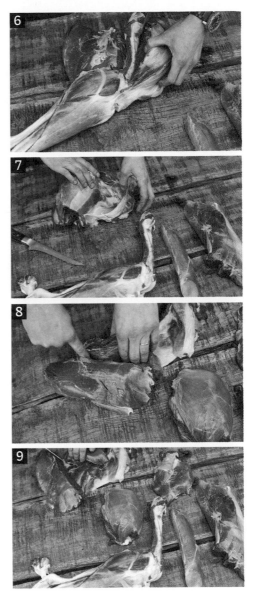

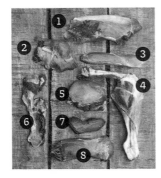

## BACK HAUNCH CUTS

| | |
|---|---|
| 1 Silverside | 5 D-joint |
| 2 Rump | 6 Scrag |
| 3 Salmon fillet | 7 Bullet |
| 4 Shank | 8 Fat flank or pavé |

# DEER CUTS & HOW TO USE THEM

Once a deer is broken down into its primal cuts, it can be broken down further by doing seam butchery on the back haunch to split up the different muscle groups and, to a certain extent, on the front haunch as well. Here's a simple guide to the different cuts and how they are best used in the kitchen.

## Slow cooking, stewing and mincing

For all your stews, chillies, ragus or burgers. Shoulders can be broken down and minced or deboned, stuffed and rolled. Whatever you do with these cuts, they are hardworking muscles and therefore need slow cooking. If you're mincing these cuts, be sure to add in 20 per cent fat content. You can do this by calculating twenty per cent of the final weight of the deer mince and adding that amount in bone marrow or other fat through the mincer.

Forequarter offcuts (scrag) **(1)**
Neck **(2)**
Shoulder **(3)**
Flank **(4)**
Shank **(11)**
Hindquarter offcuts (scrag) **(14)**

## Quick cooking, rare and raw

For a quick sear or served nice and rare, these are the most tender cuts on a deer. They're perfect for tartares and carpaccio.

Pencil fillet (true fillet) **(5)**
Backstrap (fillet/saddle) **(6)**

## Good-quality steak cuts for quick cooking

While you can cook a whole back haunch, you will find a treasure trove of meaty goodness once you break down the muscle groups into separate cuts. Some of the finest textures and flavours are to be found hidden within the haunch and you can make your meat go a lot further. They are all great for kebabs, grilling, cooking and curing.

Rump **(7)**
D-joint **(8)**
Silverside **(9)**
Salmon fillet **(10)**
Fat flank **(12)**
Bullet **(13)**

## Bones (ribs, spine, pelvis, etc.)

Used for stock, stew, broth and jus. We like to make the most out of all the deer carcasses we go through. All the remaining bones are rich in collagen, cartilage and marrow and even have the odd morsel of meat still attached. They do need a bit of treatment first, so roast them before using.

For our stock at HGC, we roast these bones over the fire or in the oven to caramelize the natural sugars and get a bit of colour on them. Follow this with a long, slow simmer covered in water with the holy trinity of celery, onion and carrot, a selection of herbs (such as bay leaf, rosemary, sage and thyme) and a little seasoning. Cook for 5–6 hours, strain off the liquid into another pan and simmer to reduce. Skim off any fat or surface scum as you go. Use fresh or freeze for later use.

## DEER CUTS

1 Forequarter offcuts (scrag)
2 Neck
3 Shoulder
4 Flank
5 Pencil fillet (true fillet)
6 Backstrap (fillet/saddle)
7 Rump
8 D-joint
9 Silverside
10 Salmon fillet
11 Shank
12 Fat flank
13 Bullet
14 Hindquarter offcuts (scrag)

TIP

*Of course, you can save yourself having to do any butchery and cook the deer whole — just make sure to take out the pencil fillets first as a quick snack, get plenty of friends over to eat it and follow the Asador instructions on page 26.*

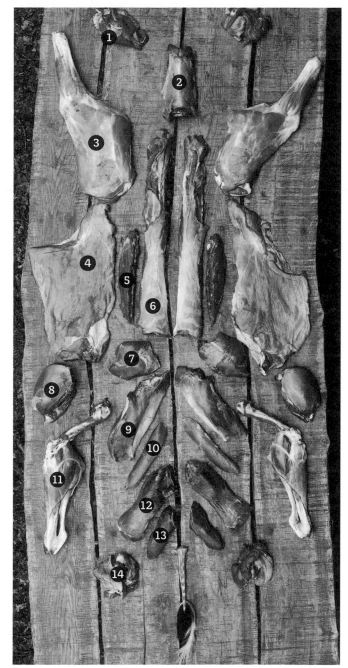

# SMOKED VENISON TARTARE

Tartare is my desert-island dish. If I go to any restaurant and it's on the menu, I will order it. While it is often pre-mixed for you when served, it is not uncommon that it will come deconstructed, with all the ingredients laid out, allowing for a spot of DIY. The best way to enjoy this dish is by spooning the different toppings off the plate and into the preserving jar. You can also spoon some of the tartare out and sprinkle it with the toppings so that every mouthful is unique.

*Serves 4*

## Ingredients

400g/14oz venison pencil fillets
or backstrap, trimmed
4 tbsp finely chopped capers
4 tbsp finely chopped
cornichons (gherkins)
4 tbsp finely chopped shallots
4 tbsp finely chopped ground
ivy or parsley leaves

4 tbsp finely chopped three-
cornered leek or wild garlic
(ramps)
4 tsp peeled and freshly grated
wild horseradish
4 tsp Dijon mustard
4 quail egg yolks, plus extra
if needed
salt and freshly ground
black pepper

## Equipment

smoke gun
4 preserving jars
4 small presentation rings, for
inside the preserving jars
woodchips

---

**The most tender cut is best for tartare, so definitely go with the pencil fillets. They are pretty much designed for a small dish like this, although the back-end of the backstrap will also do a fine job.**

For a bit of theatrical flair when serving this dish, we add some smoke to the proceedings. A smoke gun might seem a touch over the top for a kitchen in the middle of the woods, but it does have some useful applications. We originally got one for adding smoke to some wild cocktails, but then tried using it to tart up our tartare with a delicate smoky finish.

## Method

Hand mince the pencil fillets by slicing them into strips with the grain of the meat and then slicing them into small rough cubes about 5mm (¼in) thick against the grain. Put in a bowl and chill in the fridge for 15–20 minutes.

Evenly divide and neatly arrange the capers, cornichons, shallots, ground ivy and three-cornered leek onto four serving plates. Also add the wild horseradish and mustard.

Remove the meat from the fridge and season with salt and pepper. Put the presentation rings in the preserving jars and divide the minced fillet into the rings, pushing down with a spoon to make compact. Make a small well in the middle of the meat to drop the quail yolks into.

Over a bowl, crack the quail eggs, one at a time, and jiggle the yolk between your fingers to remove the egg white. Place a yolk on top of the meat in each jar, using a spoon, and season with salt.

Fill your smoke gun with woodchips (bourbon-soaked oak and cherry are our favourites), then turn on the gun and light it. Put the pipe into the top of a preserving jar and cover partially with the lid to keep the smoke in. Completely fill the chamber with smoke and then quickly pull out the pipe, seal the jar and repeat with the remaining jars.

Let the smoke sit in the jars for at least 1 minute, then put them on the prepared plates and serve. It's a very satisfying moment to watch someone's face when they pop open the jar to reveal the smoked tartare.

# CARPACCIO

Sometimes it's important to lose all the fluff and let the meat do the talking. For our carpaccio, we like to keep it basic and add just a few complementary flavourings prior to searing. You can add Parmesan shavings, a drizzle of olive oil, a little lemon juice and more seasoning, if you like, but sometimes simplicity can be an awesome thing. As long as you use the most tender cuts of the best venison you can get, you will be in a very, very good place.

*Serves 4*

## Ingredients

1 heaped tbsp Dijon mustard
2 venison pencil fillets or ½ backstrap,
    trimmed
1 handful of ground ivy, finely chopped
1 tsp freshly grated wild horseradish
1 tbsp olive oil, for searing
salt and freshly ground black pepper
crusty bread, to serve

## Method

Rub the mustard all over the fillet, then roll the fillet in the ground ivy and wild horseradish and season generously with salt and pepper. Set aside.

Heat a cast-iron frying pan or plancha (griddle) over a high heat. When it's nice and hot, add the oil, which will give off a little smoke when it's ready, then add the fillet and sear for a maximum of 1 minute on each side, just to get a bit of colour on the outside. Remove from the heat, transfer to a baking tray or large plate and put it straight in the fridge to chill for about 15 minutes.

Take the fillet out of the fridge and slice it as finely as you can – 5mm (¼in) thick is perfect. Arrange on a board or plate and serve with crusty bread.

# DIRTY PLAITED FILLET WITH PARSNIP PUREE & SORREL VERDE

This is dirty cooking at its most indulgent. A whole backstrap or fillet, trimmed, plaited (braided) and seared directly on hot coals will draw a sharp intake of breath from most fire-juggling meat aficionados.

*Serves 4*

## Ingredients

1 whole fallow backstrap or back haunch cuts, such as silverside or fat flank, about 600–800g/1lb 5oz–1lb 12oz, trimmed
1 tbsp olive oil
salt and freshly ground black pepper

### For the Sorrel Verde

1 small bunch of sorrel leaves (about 30 medium-sized leaves), finely chopped
1 small bunch of wild mint, such as water mint or spearmint, finely chopped
1 bunch of wild garlic (ramps) leaves (about 20 leaves), finely chopped
1 small bunch of parsley leaves, finely chopped
1 small bunch of basil leaves, finely chopped
60g/2¼oz anchovy fillets
60g/2¼oz/⅓ cup drained capers
2 tsp Dijon mustard
1 tbsp red wine vinegar
3 tbsp olive oil

### For the Parsnip Puree

450g/1lb parsnips, peeled, trimmed and finely sliced
240ml/8fl oz/1 cup single cream (light cream)
120ml/4fl oz/½ cup whole milk
2 garlic cloves, peeled and finely chopped
2 tbsp butter

## Equipment

butcher's string
digital thermometer
hand blender

Plaited meat is great for marinating because the strands easily get well coated in the marinade prior to plaiting and searing. Each slice gives you three little chunks of meat, which makes it simple to portion out when serving. As for three things that work together in beautiful harmony, this dish is it.

## Method

First, get your charcoal or logs on the go to establish a really good bed of embers to cook on. Once this is fired up, make the sorrel verde by putting the chopped herbs, anchovies, capers, mustard, vinegar and oil in a bowl. Season with salt and pepper and mix well, then cover and set it aside in the fridge for up to 2 hours to let the flavours mingle.

For the parsnip puree, put the parsnips in a saucepan with the cream, milk, garlic and butter. Bring to the boil, then reduce the heat to medium-low, cover and cook for 15 minutes, or until the parsnips are soft. Uncover and cook for a further 7 minutes until the liquid has reduced by half, then, using a hand blender, blend until smooth and creamy. Season to taste with salt and pepper and set aside. Reheat before serving, if necessary.

For the plaited fillet, lay the fillet on the chopping board. Starting from about 2.5cm (1in) down from the thickest end and running the knife all the way to the end, make two long cuts down the fillet to make three strands. Put the fillet in a bowl, give it a good splash of oil and season well with salt. To plait the fillet, cross each side strand over the middle strand, alternating left and right as you go and keeping the strands nice and tight. Repeat until you reach the end, then tie the loose end with butcher's string.

Once you have a good bed of embers or half burnt log, fan it with a tray or something similar to blow off the ash and reveal a red-hot cooking surface. Put the fillet directly on the hot coals and sear for 5 minutes, then flip it over onto another section of red hot embers and cook for another 3 minutes, or until the meat reaches an even internal temperature of 55°C/131°F for medium rare. Remove the fillet from the heat, dust off any clinging embers and wrap in foil to rest for 5 minutes before slicing and serving. Alternatively, you can use a conventional home cooker (stove) to sear the fillet in a hot pan over a high heat for the same amount of time. Serve with the warm parsnip puree and topped with the sorrel verde.

# VENISON BURGERS

The deer is a very lean animal, so having enough fat content can sometimes be a struggle. With the flank, you do get a certain amount of fat content and sometimes on the back haunches you will get a good slab of fat covering the meat, but most of the time you will have to add fat content where needed. The perfect burger should be around 80 per cent meat to 20 per cent fat, taking into account what you get from the flank. We also add in bone marrow for a truly flavourful burger.

*Serves 4*

# Ingredients

## For the Burgers

1 tbsp olive oil

1 onion, peeled and finely chopped

800g/1lb 12oz minced venison (ground venison), preferably shoulder and flank

80g/2¾oz bone marrow

4 tsp ground ivy, finely chopped

4 slices of Cheddar cheese

salt

## To serve

4 brioche burger buns (brioche rolls or hamburger rolls)

8 tbsp Smoke-roasted Wild Garlic Mayo (see page 212)

a few lettuce leaves

2 tomatoes, sliced

1 red onion, peeled and sliced into rings

2–3 pickles, sliced lengthwise

4 tbsp Proper Horseradish Sauce (see page 164)

# Equipment

mincer

---

A mincer can really help to make the most out of a whole deer. We primarily tend to mince the shoulders and flanks and any other scraps such as the scrag, intercostal muscles, neck offcuts and anything else that cannot be used as a whole cut. You can buy a fairly inexpensive mincer or, if you want to go back to basics, get yourself a hand mincer and use some elbow grease as we did at the start of HGC.

# Method

Heat the oil in a small frying pan over a medium heat, add the onion, cover and cook, stirring occasionally, for 10–15 minutes until the onion is softened and translucent. Then set aside to cool completely.

While the onion is cooking, pass the minced venison and bone marrow through the mincer, using a coarse plate, so that the bone marrow is well broken up. Put it in a bowl.

Add the onion and ground ivy to the mince and mix thoroughly. Divide the mince mixture into four equal portions of 220g/7¾oz each. Using your hands, shape each portion into a ball and then flatten into a 2.5cm (1in) thick burger. Put them on a plate and season with a little salt.

Heat a heavy cast-iron pan or heavy frying pan over a high heat. Put the burgers in the pan and, trying not to move them around, cook for 4–5 minutes until a solid crust starts to develop, then flip them over. Once flipped, immediately put the Cheddar slices on top. If possible, cover the pan with a lid to help melt the cheese and cook for a further 3–4 minutes.

Meanwhile, toast the brioche buns by the fire or in another pan.

Once cooked to your liking, build your burgers. Put the bottom of a brioche bun on each of four plates and add the toppings of your choice. We go for the mayo on the bottom, then the lettuce, burger, tomato, onion rings, pickles and a final flourish of wild horseradish sauce, then cover with the tops of the buns and serve. Good stuff indeed.

# DIRTY DOE TACOS

We are all huge fans of Mexican food down at HGC and tacos are one of our favourites. If they have venison in them, then all the better. These tacos make for an awesome barbecue dish and a surefire crowd pleaser. This recipe calls for a bit of dirty cooking (see page 34). It doesn't matter if you are using venison from a buck or a doe, the name Dirty Doe just has a good ring to it.

*Serves 6*

## Ingredients

20 small corn tortillas, about
    10–12cm/4–5in in diameter
2 fat flanks or 1 backstrap, trimmed
salt and freshly ground black pepper
1 recipe quantity Guacamole (see page
    69), to serve
1 recipe quantity Burnt Ash Salsa
    (see page 157), to serve

### For the HGC Slaw

½ red cabbage, finely sliced
1 large red onion, peeled and
    finely sliced
1 cucumber, quartered, deseeded and
    finely sliced
10 radishes, very finely sliced
1 red chilli, deseeded and finely sliced
1 small bunch of coriander (cilantro)
    leaves, chopped
juice of 1 lime
1 tbsp apple cider vinegar
2 tbsp olive oil

### Equipment

digital thermometer

## Method

To make the slaw, put the cabbage, onion, cucumber, radishes, chilli and coriander in a large bowl, season with salt and pepper and toss well. In a small bowl, mix together the lime juice, vinegar and oil and set aside until about 10 minutes before serving. When ready to serve, add the dressing to the slaw and toss well.

Get your charcoal on the go to prepare for your dirty cooking. When they are red hot, flatten out a bed for the venison and fan any ash off the embers. Wrap the tortillas in foil and put them near the coals to warm through.

Season the cuts of venison with salt and put them directly on the hot coals for a good sear. Remember it's all about the temperature, not the timing. Check the venison to see if it's forming a good crust and then flip it over onto a fresh patch of coals. You are looking for an even internal temperature of 55°C/131°F for medium rare, which you can check using a digital thermometer. Once you hit this point, take the venison off and dust off any clinging embers. Wrap it in foil and leave to rest for 5 minutes, then slice the meat and let everyone build their own tacos, adding the slaw, guacamole and salsa.

*TIP*
*Dressing the slaw just before serving helps to ensure the slaw stays crunchy and fresh. Adding the dressing too early can make it a bit soft and watery.*

# HUEVOS RANCHEROS

There is simply no better way to start off the day than with this 'full English' interpretation of huevos rancheros. If you are looking for a hearty breakfast, this recipe delivers on all fronts. The venison chilli can be cooked ahead, as can the burnt ash salsa, and then it's just a case of assembling it all. We tend to put it all in a cast-iron pan, drop in the eggs and bake it in the clay oven (see page 28), then add the guacamole, chillies and coriander.

*Serves 4*

# Ingredients

2 tbsp butter

1 tbsp vegetable oil

1 large onion, peeled and
finely diced

1 handful of wild garlic (ramps)
or 4 garlic cloves, peeled and
finely chopped

1 red pepper, deseeded and
finely chopped

2 dried ancho chillies,
rehydrated in hot water and
finely chopped

1 handful of coriander (cilantro),
leaves and stems separated
and finely chopped

500g/1lb 2oz minced venison
(ground venison), preferably
a mix of flank and shoulder

4 large tomatoes, finely
chopped

1 x 400g/14oz can of kidney
beans, drained and rinsed to
yield 240g/8oz/1 cup beans

1 tbsp Worcestershire sauce

1 tbsp ground cumin

2 bay leaves

1 beef stock cube (beef bouillon
cube)

4 corn tortillas, cut in half

4 eggs

4–5 tbsp Burnt Ash Salsa
(see page 157), plus extra
to serve

150g/5½oz feta cheese, drained
and rinsed, broken into
small pieces

salt and freshly ground black
pepper

1 green chilli, finely sliced,
to serve

## For the Guacamole

2 large avocados, halved and
stones (pits) removed

juice of 1 lime

---

There is no way to serve this in a refined fashion.
Wedges of it will do, dollops are even better, or
just give everyone a spoon. No other breakfast
makes your axe swing as well as this does....

# Method

To make the chilli, heat a large pan over a
medium-high heat. Add the butter and oil, then
add the onions, wild garlic, red pepper, ancho
chillies and coriander stems. Fry for 5 minutes,
stirring frequently, until the onions soften and
take on a bit of colour. Add the venison mince
and cook, moving it around the pan for about
5 minutes until it gets a bit of colour on it.

Add the tomatoes, kidney beans, Worcestershire
sauce, cumin, bay leaves and stock cube and
season with salt and pepper. Stir well and drop
the heat down to a gentle simmer. Stir every 5–10
minutes and season to taste, then cook gently
for at least 1 hour, until it has reduced nicely and
taken on a rich, dark colour.

Shortly before the chilli is done cooking and you
are ready to eat, make the guacamole. Using a
spoon, scoop out the avocado flesh and put it in
a medium-sized bowl. Add the lime juice and
season with salt. Mash together with a fork until
you have a nice chunky texture.

When you are ready to assemble the huevos
rancheros, preheat the oven to 180°C/350°F/gas
mark 4. Arrange the tortilla halves in a cast-iron
pan or baking dish, overlapping them slightly,
and ladle in the venison chilli. Crack the eggs into
a small bowl, then pour them over the top of the
chilli. Add 4–5 tablespoons of the burnt ash salsa
and sprinkle the feta cheese over the top.

Put the pan in the oven and bake for 5 minutes
until the eggs have nearly cooked through but the
yolks are still soft. Remove from the oven and top
with the guacamole. Sprinkle with the coriander
leaves and green chilli and serve with extra salsa.

"Taking the responsibility of where your meat comes from and how it has ended up in your kitchen is one of the most important lessons we can learn in the 21st century..."

# RABBIT

Of all the quarry species in this book, I would say I have a lot to thank the rabbit for. It was the first wild animal I shot for the pot and it instilled in me a passion for hunting and the virtues of wild meat. I think the part that drew me in was the self-sufficiency of it all: the experience of stalking a rabbit and gradually figuring out the actions and behaviour of such wild creatures and how they could eventually end up in the pan and on the plate if you mastered the equation. In essence it's the same story around the globe: what makes people hunt?

**H**UNTING IS SOMETHING THAT is naturally encoded into our DNA; we are and always will be hunters. These days some people suppress the natural urge and choose not to do it, and others vehemently oppose and protest against it. We are all entitled to our opinions and lifestyle choices: the fact that these are 'options' in this day and age is a sign of just how easy we have it today. Protein sources come in a wealth of different packages these days. Unless you are exposed to hunting at a young age, the separation between meat from a supermarket and an animal 'skin on' in its natural packaging is not entirely clear. Taking the responsibility of where your meat comes from and how it has ended up in your kitchen is one of the most important lessons we can learn in the 21st century and for me, as a father, exposing my young son to it is something I feel strongly about. I want him to have a clear connection of where his meat comes from and what it actually looks like.

Growing up in the heart of the Ashdown Forest in Sussex, hunting was something we just did. The fact I had a brother who was five years older than me certainly helped. He was the one who taught me how to shoot an air rifle, how to stalk a rabbit and how to skin and gut one. I got my first air rifle when I was twelve. It was my pride and joy, but it also taught me about responsibility. This was something that had the potential to cause real harm and had to be treated with respect.

The first time I shot a rabbit with it was in the fields of a manor house near to where I lived. I wasn't allowed to shoot on their land, but convinced myself that pest control was a good excuse if caught. I still remember the moment of impact: the way the rabbit was literally flattened by the clean headshot I had spent 20 minutes getting into the right position to take. My head had been clear up to the moment I flicked off the safety and pulled the trigger. What I wasn't prepared for was the emotions that would follow. I had bashed a trout over the head before when out fly-fishing with my father and not shown much remorse, but this felt very different: excitement and sadness at the same time. I remember being slightly tearful and not really knowing if I'd done something that was right or wrong. It was one of those salient points in my early days and it was then and there that I made the conscious decision that I would not take an animal's life if I was not prepared to eat it. It would be fair to say, even up to this day, that it was the best rabbit I've ever tasted.

What I did learn that day was respect. Respect for the animal is a key part of hunting. The first time I shot a deer many years later I had a brief flurry of similar feelings, which as an adult I recognized as a good thing. All the animals we hunt for the table are beautiful creatures and a joy to observe in the wild. To strip one of its life is a conscious decision that we make, and it is our responsibility to ensure it is done cleanly and efficiently.

don't require a firearms licence to purchase or own. Ferreting is also a good way to obtain rabbits and is a great sport to get into if you have the time to do it. Shotguns work, but they don't leave much of a useful rabbit for the kitchen. Getting access to land for shooting rabbits is not that difficult. Most landowners or farmers will certainly want ridding of them, so it is really about asking around. Someone will always know someone. As ever, common decency is a great form of bartering for shooting rights: bottles of things or culinary creations of their very own rabbits is a good exchange rate.

In terms of eating, rabbits are wonderfully versatile and fairly mild in flavour. The majority of a rabbit needs the slow cook or confit treatment, being incredibly lean and quite a hardworking bundle of muscles, apart from the fillets or loin which, once trimmed, can be quick cooked or served up as a seared carpaccio. They need to be used within a few days of shooting – they certainly don't benefit from prolonged hanging.

As a hunter, having a slight sense of remorse is not a bad thing; it's part of being human. Although to be fair, the animals we hunt do have one major downfall, which is the very reason that we pursue them: they taste pretty darned good.

Right, so now we've covered my ethical stance on hunting, we'll move on: rabbits. If you want to get into shooting, rabbits are the entry-level quarry of choice. We're not short of rabbits; they spread like wildfire. In the space of a year a doe (female) can have several litters of between 4–8 kits (bunnies). That's an awful lot of bunnies to be dealing with, and the damage they cause to agriculture is astounding, so naturally in order to protect such valuable crops, ethical pest control is the best option. This of course opens up a huge amount of excellent quality wild meat and one which most farmers or landowners are very willing to be rid of.

Most rabbit shooting is done with a rifle or air rifle. Air rifles are a lot more accessible as they

## DISEASES IN RABBITS
Despite the large rabbit population we have today, there have certainly been troughs. In 1953, a man-made disease called myxomatosis came to the UK. Originally used in Australia for rabbit control, it was devastating, wiping out almost 90 per cent of the rabbit population by 1955. Gradually rabbits have recovered but you do find myxomatosis still occurs in pockets here and there. Now there is also a form of chronic wasting disease that is appearing in wild populations of rabbits – you will know if you've shot one that has it because the rabbit will be mostly skin and bones. It should be returned to the hedgerow for the foxes.

# RABBIT BUTCHERY

Breaking down a rabbit is quite a bit quicker than doing a deer, but essentially they have the same body structure. You can even break down a rabbit haunch into exactly the same cuts mentioned on pages 54–55. Once you get used to the process, a rabbit can be skinned and jointed in less than 5 minutes.

Paunching or gutting the rabbit is the first thing to do. First, 'pee' the rabbit by rubbing your thumb on its abdomen to get rid of urine from its bladder. Then, take a pinch of its belly between thumb and forefinger and gently cut in with a knife, taking care not to cut into the intestines. Once opened, use your fingers to open it up even more, then lay the rabbit on its side and draw out the innards until they are disconnected. Liver, kidneys and heart are the best bits of offal to use. If the liver is deep red and has no small white bumps, it's good for eating.

**1** Start by cutting off the tail and removing all four feet just above the joints in the legs, using a cleaver, secateurs or axe.

**2** Remove the head just above the shoulders with a machete/axe combo by gently tapping on the back of the axe with a machete. You can also use a chef's knife, although it will take a bit more work.

**3** To start the skinning process, make what we call the 'bunny handbag'. Separate the pelt from the belly skin on both sides and work around to the back so it is released. Then work the pelt back towards the hind legs.

**4** The bunny handbag may sound like a strange way to describe this stage of the process, but we have found on our courses that it sticks in the attendees' heads for future reference.

**5** Pop out the rabbit's knees and pull the skin off each back leg so that only the anal tract is still attached to the skin. Slice through this with a knife to release.

**6** Grip the rabbit by the waist and take a firm hold of the skin. Gradually draw the skin off the rest of the rabbit until it pops off the neck and front legs. Any 'socks' left on the legs can be removed by hand or with a knife.

**7** To remove the shoulders, lay the rabbit on its back, open up the shoulder with thumb and forefinger and slice down the side of the ribcage until it is detached. Repeat on the other shoulder.

**8** To remove the back haunches, use your knife to score around the shape of the back haunch from the outside of the leg to the inside, right against the pelvis. Once you have cut right to the bone, you can pop out the ball and socket and remove the back haunch. Repeat on the other haunch.

**9** To begin removing the fillets, use the knife to cut into the bottom of the fillet along the inside of the pelvis, which runs at a 45-degree angle. Let the bone structure be the guide for your knife. This will then release the end of the fillet.

**10** Along the spine of the rabbit are two visible white lines of membrane. Run your knife down the length of these from the back end of the fillet where you separated it from the pelvis. Keep slicing, then roll the fillet off the ribcage with your fingers until it thins out up by the shoulder. Repeat with the other fillet. Once the fillets are off, trim off the fine white membrane on both of them before cooking.

**11** Finally, tear the diaphragm inside the ribcage and pull out the heart and lungs. Hearts make for a tasty grilled treat. The carcass is great for stock, the shoulders and back haunches for slow cooking and the fillets for a quick cook. You can remove all the meat from the back haunches and mince it for burgers or ragu – just make sure you add in some bone marrow or some sort of fat before cooking.

# RABBIT CARPACCIO

I sometimes call this dish 'rabaccio'. It's one of the first things I do with a glut of freshly shot spring bunnies. Not many people are aware that rabbit can be eaten virtually raw but it can as long as the rabbit used is fresh, young and in good condition. If you are partial to meat in the raw, this is definitely one to try. The texture is amazing and the mustard emulsion gives it a bit of a wasabi-like hit of heat. Served with pickled carrot and a few leaves from the wild, this is the hedgerow, served straight up.

*Serves 2*

## Ingredients

4 rabbit fillets, trimmed
1 handful of parsley leaves,
    finely chopped
1 handful of ground ivy, finely chopped
2 tsp English mustard
1½ tsp olive oil
salt and freshly ground black pepper
2 handfuls of wild leaves, such as
    baby sorrel and cuckoo flower
    (lady's smock) to serve
a few ground ivy flowers to serve

### For the Pickled Carrots

1 carrot, peeled and thinly shaved
2 tbsp tarragon vinegar or apple
    cider vinegar

## Method

To make the pickled carrots, put the carrot in a small bowl, add a little salt and mix well, then add the tarragon vinegar and put in the fridge for 30 minutes to 1 hour to pickle. When done pickling, remove the carrot from the liquid and drain on a paper towel.

Put the parsley and ground ivy in a bowl and season with salt and pepper. Roll each rabbit fillet through the herb mixture until well coated, then wrap them up tightly in plastic wrap, twisting the ends until you have a firm sausage. Put them in the fridge for 10 minutes before cooking, or for up to 6 hours. Put the mustard and olive oil in a small bowl and mix well.

Heat a pan over a high heat, or use a plancha (griddle). When it's almost smoking, remove the plastic wrap from the fillets and drop the fillets straight on. Sear on all sides for 1–2 minutes, to give them some light colour. Remove the fillets and slice them across the grain into 5mm (¼in) thick rounds.

Spoon the mustard emulsion onto two plates, put the pickled carrot on top and then add the rabbit slices. Season with salt and pepper and serve with the wild leaves and flowers.

*TIP*
*You can use a vegetable peeler or a box grater with a slicer on it to shave the carrot in this recipe.*

# ROLLED RABBIT FILLETS WITH PICKLED BURDOCK ROOT & STINGER NETTLE PESTO CAKES

A long-standing favourite on the HGC summer menu, this recipe has evolved and developed over time but its two essential ingredients, rabbit and nettle, always remain the focus. This version features two other ingredients that rabbit is particularly happy to work with on the plate: mustard and sage. Pair them with your rabbits and they will dance across your palette, just like they would across a field, right before they start their journey towards the kitchen.

*Serves 4*

# Ingredients

8 slices of pancetta

4 tsp Dijon mustard

16 sage leaves, plus a few extra
   for serving

4 rabbit fillets, trimmed

1 tbsp olive oil, plus extra for
   drizzling

freshly ground black pepper

a few three-cornered leek
   flowers, to serve

1 recipe quantity Stinger Nettle
   Pesto Cakes (see page 166),
   shaped into 4 burgers,
   to serve

## For the Pickled Burdock Root

1 burdock root, peeled and
   finely sliced

1 recipe quantity HGC Pickling
   Liquid (see page 168)

2 tbsp soy sauce

# Equipment

small preserving jar (about
   240ml/8fl oz/1 cup)

digital thermometer

---

**Pickled burdock root is a larder staple for us, but if you don't have it to hand, you can use carrot, broccoli or asparagus instead. It is, however, easy to make.**

# Method

To make the pickled burdock, put all of the ingredients in a preserving jar, seal and leave to stand for 1 week.

Lay out two slices of pancetta diagonally on your chopping board and spread one quarter of the mustard across them. Space four of the sage leaves out across the pancetta and season with pepper. Put the fat end of one of the rabbit fillets at the bottom end of the pancetta slices and then roll it up tightly in the pancetta. Repeat with the remaining pancetta, sage leaves and rabbit fillets until you have four ready to go.

Heat up a heavy cast-iron pan or grill over a medium-high heat, add 2 teaspoons of the oil and put the rolled fillets into the pan. Sear for 2–3 minutes until golden brown on the outside, slightly firm to the touch and the internal temperature reaches 50°C/131°F on a digital thermometer. Wrap in foil and leave to rest for 5 minutes.

In the same pan, heat the remaining 1 teaspoon of the oil. Add the nettle pesto cakes and fry for 1–2 minutes on each side. Then add the pickled burdock root and fry, stirring occasionally, until it starts to colour.

To serve, slice each fillet in half at an angle. Put one pesto cake on the centre of each plate and top with the sliced fillets. Serve with the pickled burdock root, extra sage leaves, the three-cornered leek flowers and a drizzle of oil.

# BUNNY SLIDERS

This mini burger is so deliciously decadent, it deserves a starring role in the fast food arena. Bone marrow provides essential fat content and the extra components really raise the bar. You will be chomping at the grass for more.

*Serves 4*

## Ingredients

300g/10½oz minced rabbit (ground rabbit), from deboned back haunches
60g/2¼oz bone marrow
1 handful of ground ivy, finely chopped
4 slices of Monterey Jack cheese
salt

### For the Quick-pickled Red Onion

1 red onion, peeled and sliced into thin rounds
2 tbsp red wine vinegar

### To serve

4 small brioche burger buns (brioche rolls or hamburger rolls)
4 romaine lettuce leaves
hot sauce
6 tbsp Smoke-roasted Wild Garlic Mayo (see page 160), plus extra if desired
1 recipe quantity Ground Ivy Rosti (see page 99)

## Equipment

blowtorch
mincer

## Method

To make the pickle, put the red onion and vinegar in a bowl, sprinkle with a little salt and stir well. Chill in the fridge for 30 minutes.

Pass the mince and bone marrow through the mincer, using a fine plate, so the bone marrow is well broken up, then mix together thoroughly in a bowl with the ground ivy. Using your hands, shape the meat mixture into four equal-sized sliders about 2cm (¾in) thick and 9cm (3½in) in diameter. Season the sliders with a little salt and heat a cast-iron pan over a high heat. Put the sliders in the pan and cook for 3–4 minutes until a solid crust starts to develop. Try not to move them around. Flip the sliders and immediately top them with the cheese slices and let the cheese melt a bit. Meanwhile, toast the brioche buns by the fire or in your pan.

When the sliders are nearly done, light a blowtorch and finish off the melting process by hand. Try to get a bit of colour on the cheese.

To construct the sliders, lay down the bottoms of the buns and assemble from the ground up. Spread half of the mayo over the buns, add the lettuce, then the sliders. Add some hot sauce, the rosti cakes and the pickled onion and finish with the rest of the mayo. Cover with the tops of the buns and serve.

*TIP*
*If you don't have time to make the rosti cakes, hash browns work equally well as a quick fix.*

# CONFIT RABBIT

You can't have a book based on game and not cover the age-old technique of confit. Whether it's rabbit legs, duck legs, partridge legs or pheasant legs, the confit treatment gives these hard-working, incredibly lean cuts a gentle, luxurious massage of fatty goodness and renders them succulently rich and delightfully moreish.

*TIP*

*If you are going to use the confit straight away or within 3 days, you can use vegetable oil in this recipe. For longer-term storage of up to 1 month, use duck fat.*

*Serves 4*

# Ingredients

8 rabbit legs

160g/6¼oz/heaping ¾ cup fine
    sea salt

800g/1lb 12oz/scant 4 cups
    duck fat or 435ml/15¼fl oz/1¾
    cups vegetable oil, plus extra
    if needed

1 small handful of wild garlic
    (ramps) leaves and scapes,
    or 1 head of garlic, crushed
    and cloves separated

1 bunch of sage leaves

3 sprigs of rosemary

1 small bunch of fennel fronds

5 bay leaves

10 black peppercorns

1 lemon, halved, to serve

1 tsp olive oil

# Equipment

digital thermometer, if using
    a clay oven

large preserving jar, if storing
    the confit

---

It may seem a bit complicated to begin with, but I can assure you the process is quite straightforward and makes excellent use of the not-so-prime cuts from game birds and bunnies. A quick dry cure at the start prepares the rabbit legs here for their rendezvous with the fat. Duck fat is preferable, but vegetable oil works as well, though it is not recommended for long-term storage. Aromatics are completely up to you and add a subtle background to the finished product. You can use these in so many ways. Try them in tacos and with pasta or curry, or experiment by adding them to some of your other favourite dishes.

## Method

Put the rabbit legs on a baking tray and evenly sprinkle the salt over them. Cover and chill in the fridge for 3 hours, then rinse and pat dry with paper towels. Preheat the oven to 120°C/250°F/gas mark ½ or, if using a clay oven (see page 28), make sure the temperature stays between 100–120°C/200–250°F throughout cooking by checking it with a digital thermometer.

Put the duck fat or oil in a deep oven tray and add the wild garlic, sage, rosemary, fennel, bay leaves and peppercorns. Put the rabbit legs on top and make sure everything is well submerged in the

fat. Add more fat if necessary. Carefully put the tray in the oven and leave the fat to work its magic for the next 4 hours or until everything falls off the bone. When the rabbit is falling off the bone, take the tray out of the oven and leave to cool slightly, then gently remove each leg and drain them on paper towels.

Put some of the duck fat or oil from the baking tray into a preserving jar while it is still liquid. Add all of the rabbit legs and top up with more of the fat until the legs are completely submerged. Leave to cool and set, then put the jar in the fridge.

We serve these confit legs with grilled lemon, having given them a flash in a hot pan to caramelize the outside of the meat. Preheat the grill (broiler) to a medium-high setting, put the lemon, cut-sides up, on a baking tray and grill for 3–4 minutes until beginning to brown. If you have a barbecue going, simply put the lemon halves, cut-side down, on the grill for a couple of minutes till they have some colour and smoke.

Heat a pan over a medium-high heat, add the olive oil then add the rabbit legs. Cook for 3–4 minutes, turning occasionally, until browned on both sides. Serve with a squeeze of the grilled lemon.

# RABBIT QUESADILLAS

Quesadillas can lay claim to being one of the greatest food inventions ever. Spicy, meaty, oozing with cheese and with a slight crisp on the outside, they are beautiful things. The most important thing in making perfect quesadillas is to have your *mise en place* on point: have all ingredients ready to go, then crack through the construction and cooking process in one fell swoop.

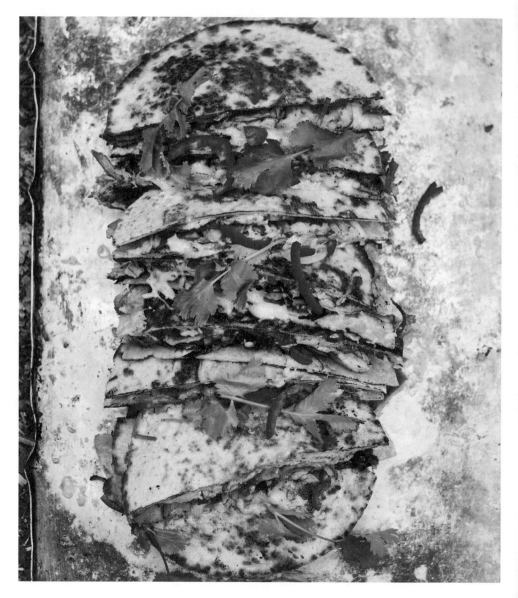

*Serves 4*

# Ingredients

½ recipe quantity Confit Rabbit
(see page 82)
2 tbsp olive oil
8 corn tortillas
400g/14oz/3⅓ cups grated
Cheddar cheese
1 green pepper, finely sliced
1 red onion, peeled and
finely sliced
4 tbsp Lacto-fermented Wild
Garlic (see page 163)

a small bunch of coriander
(cilantro) leaves
a small handful of water pepper
(arsemart) leaves
1 red chilli, finely sliced
salt

## For the HGC Mexican rub

1 tsp cumin
1 tsp salt
1 tsp chilli flakes
2 tsp smoked dried wild garlic
(ramps) scapes (see Smoked
Wild Garlic Salt, page 162)
1 tsp dried oregano
1 tsp smoked paprika
1 tsp dark brown soft sugar
zest of 1 lime

Rabbit has always been a popular food in
Mexico, and archaeological evidence suggests
they were a driving force behind the ancient
city of Teotihuacan, which thrived, in part, due
to its trade in rabbit meat and fur. So 'conejo'
quesadillas have probably been around for a long
time. Make these and you will see exactly why.

# Method

In a bowl, mix together all of the ingredients for
the rub, then pick the rabbit meat off the bones
and place in another bowl. Add 2 tablespoons
of the rub to the rabbit and toss well. Add more
if desired.

Heat a pan over a medium-high heat, add
1 tablespoon of the oil and fry the rabbit pieces for
3–4 minutes, stirring frequently, to get a bit of
colour on it. Transfer the rabbit to a bowl and set
aside with the rest of the quesadilla ingredients.

Put one of the tortillas on a chopping board and
sprinkle a small handful of the cheese over it so
that it covers the entire tortilla. Add one quarter

of the rabbit, and one quarter each of the peppers,
red onion and wild garlic. Sprinkle with a few
coriander and water pepper leaves and top it off
with another small handful of the cheese. Finally,
press another tortilla firmly down on top. Repeat
with the remaining tortillas and fillings to make
four quesadillas.

Heat a heavy cast-iron pan or plancha (griddle)
over a medium-high heat, then add a little of the
remaining oil and, using a spatula, carefully place
the first quesadilla into the pan. Press it down
firmly with the spatula and cook for 3–4 minutes
until the underside of the tortilla is beginning
to brown, then flip it over. Cook for another 3–4
minutes until the cheese has melted and the
underside of the tortilla has browned. Remove
from the pan and repeat with the remaining
quesadillas, adding more oil if necessary. To
serve, cut the quesadillas in half, top with the
chilli and sprinkle with a little salt and some
coriander leaves.

# POPCORN BUNNIES

Game, in general, is never an easy sell. Despite all the pros behind it (wild, free-range, natural diet, ethically sourced, etc.), it doesn't always appeal to the general public, who often seem sceptical about consuming what, to many, is an unfamiliar meat these days. However, presenting it in a way that is familiar can dramatically sway opinion. The chicken nugget is appreciated around the world, so if you present rabbit, pheasant or partridge in a similar fashion, you have a game changer. If you are looking to get the kids into rabbit, then this is the recipe to do it with.

*Serves 3–4 as a snack or canapés*

## Ingredients

700ml/24fl oz/4 cups vegetable oil, for deep-frying
200g/7oz/1⅓ cups plain flour (all-purpose flour)
1 tsp salt
1 tsp cayenne pepper
2 eggs
200g/7oz/2⅔ cups panko breadcrumbs
8 rabbit fillets, trimmed and cut into 2.5cm/1in cubes
125g/4½oz/½ cup Smoke-roasted Wild Garlic Mayo (see page 160), plus extra if desired, to serve

## Equipment

deep fryer (optional)
digital thermometer

## Method

Put the oil into a medium saucepan and heat it over a medium heat. Take extra care if you are doing this over a fire – a deep-fat fryer or gas ring may be preferable.

Put the flour, salt and cayenne pepper in a mixing bowl and mix well. In another bowl, whisk the eggs thoroughly. Put the breadcrumbs in another bowl.

When the oil has reached 180°C/350°F, start batch cooking the popcorn bunnies. Roll a handful of the fillet cubes in the seasoned flour until well coated, then dip them in the egg and roll them around in the breadcrumbs until evenly coated. Carefully put the coated rabbit pieces into the hot oil, taking care that the oil doesn't splash. Cook for a couple of minutes or until they have turned a nice golden colour. Keep a good eye on them to prevent them from burning.

Remove the popcorn bunnies from the oil, using a slotted spoon, and drain on paper towels. Repeat with the rest of the rabbit, working in batches and taking care not to overcrowd the pan, which will massively drop the temperature of the oil.

Serve immediately with the mayo for dipping. These two things were made for one and other.

# PHEASANT & PARTRIDGE

For me, the pheasant is the hallmark of the British countryside and there are few places where you won't catch a glimpse of the iconic bird strutting his stuff, with his rusty coloured plumage and fancy white necklace. It may be a surprise for you to learn that this wonderful game bird is actually not native to the UK but is predominantly from the Far East. The shooting season for pheasants in England and Wales runs from the start of October to the beginning of February, which allows plenty of time for you to really get to grips with this fantastic bird. In other regions, check online or in your local area to find out what's in season and when.

MY FIRST INTERACTION WITH *Phasianus colchicus* was hand-feeding one we had living in our garden when I was about six or seven. Ziggy became a mainstay at our outdoor bird feeder and, after some time, became quite tame. After reading *The New Poacher's Handbook* by Ian Niall, a few years later, I learned that pheasants were apparently very tasty birds and shooting them was perfectly acceptable. My early forays into pheasant shooting were certainly not on the right side of the law, I must admit. A black widow catapult in the hands of a twelve-year-old might provide a bird or two for the pot, but it will also prompt parents to investigate the kind of literature their offspring are reading.

Of course, through the eyes of an adult, I am firmly against poaching and it is not something I would ever encourage, but those early days did teach me a healthy respect for the pheasant and a sense of excitement on encountering one, which I still have today. In fact, the pheasant in our HGC logo is called Jeff, in honour of a friendly bird that used to hang around the Treehouse I lived in for six months back in 2009.

Sometimes known as Longtails, pheasants are highly prized as sporting birds because of their ability to fly high and hold their ground. There are a number of different strains, including English Blacknecks, French Ringnecks and Michigan Bluebacks but in terms of flavour there is not much variation. Partridge is another popular game bird. Two species reside in the UK: our native grey partridge, which have been in decline since the 1940s, and the much more common and widespread red-legged or French partridge. The game season for partridge usually starts a month prior to pheasant season. As always, check your local guidelines and regulations.

In the UK, pheasants and partridge have been bred and reared specifically for shooting and their diets supplemented with grain, so they're not exactly wild birds, but they live a free-range existence and a good percentage of their diet is from the wild, including wild thyme, clover and wild marjoram. At the table, I tend to prefer the tender, somewhat sweeter flavour of partridge over the bolder, more gamey flavour of pheasant. Plus, since they're smaller, you can fit a lot more of them in your fridge and freezer.

If you enjoy your field sports, few things can be more exciting and satisfying than a well-aimed shot and bringing your quarry to hand. I do mostly rough shooting rather than large scale, professional-driven shooting (my pockets are not deep enough for the pleasure). But the rewards are plenty and accessible to all of us at an affordable price. If you yourself don't shoot or know anyone who does, going straight to source for your birds is always best in terms of freshness and cost. In the countryside, you are never more than a few miles from the nearest shoot. Get to know the local gamekeeper or estate (game farm), perhaps do a bit of beating on a shoot. It makes for a great day out. Plus, you can get paid in birds, too… Failing that, country pubs are always good places to start when trying to find out where to obtain game birds. There is always someone who knows someone who might know someone.

At HGC, it's very much about how the bird performs on the palate rather than in the air. Once you know how to process the bird, either by plucking and drawing, or skinning and boning, they are incredibly versatile in the kitchen. They can be treated in exactly the same way as chicken with one minor drawback that almost all game have on their disclaimer: a lack of fat content. This can be very problematic and lead to a tough, dry lunch. However, you can remedy this by gentle cooking and by adding fat, such as olive oil, butter, lard, bacon or pork fat. If you can find it, Iberico pork fat is by far the best

option. This wonderful stuff can be bought by the jar and contains the finest lard from the black Iberian pigs that have a penchant for acorns. We use it a lot and you will see from the recipes that follow how it can help with everything from basting a bird to blowtorching one.

Other things to take into consideration are the sex and age of the bird. Traditionally, most game birds are sold in a 'brace', which will be made up of a male and a female. Hens and young birds are more tender; older birds or male birds will need more attention, such as basting more frequently, to keep the meat from toughening up during cooking. With partridge, this can be hard to distinguish, so one trick is to use their red legs as a guide. The paler the legs, the younger the bird, and if you detect a wide bump or formation of a broader spur on the legs then it's likely to be a male. Females have more slender legs and a less pronounced, narrow leg spur, if any at all.

## HANGING GAME BIRDS

There has always been a bit of debate about how long you should hang your birds for. Gone are the days when people would wait for them to go green and have maggots falling out the bottom before deeming them fit to eat. Tradition is often in need of updating now and again.

The main reason to hang any game is to allow it to tenderize and to develop its characteristic flavour, but how long is long enough? Once the birds have been shot, it is essential to cool them as quickly as possible because the residual heat from freshly shot birds that have been bundled together can cause them to spoil at an alarming rate. Allowing them to hang with plenty of airflow or getting them to a chiller or fridge as soon as possible is key. Other factors such as age do come into play as well. The younger the bird, the less time it will need hanging. As a general rule, pheasant will need around 2–3 days at 4°C (39°F) and partridge 1–2 days at the same temperature. However, both can be dealt with as soon as they are cooled down. Let personal preference be your guide, too: the gamier you want it, the longer you hang it.

# GAME BIRD BUTCHERY

You can use the techniques below to process all game birds mentioned in this book. Most of the time, the skinning and boning method will be the most useful. It's the quickest, easiest and least messy route to getting a bird ready for the kitchen, and it allows for a lot more versatility when it comes to cooking. Plucking and drawing (removing the insides) keeps the skin intact and really only applies if you are looking to roast, spatchcock or grill the bird whole. However, you can also skin the entire bird, remove the breasts and legs, draw it and use the carcass for stock.

## Skinning and boning

**1** Lay the bird on its back. Pinch and hold the skin and feathers in the middle of the chest and gently pull up, then take a sharp knife and make a light incision, just enough to cut through the skin.

**2** Ease both of your forefingers into the incision and gently part the skin. It will come apart easily. Keep opening it up so the breasts are fully exposed and continue all the way up to expose the back legs as well.

**3** Using a finger, feel around for the breastbone. You should be able to see it quite clearly. Then, using the knife, slice from the top of the breast to the base on one side of it. The knife will only go as far as the breastplate as you cut down, but you must take care not to use too much pressure and go through to the innards. The bone structure of the bird will be your guide. Using your thumb, pull the breast away from the bird, cutting along the breastplate from top to bottom as you go until you can remove the whole breast and then repeat on the other side.

**4** To remove the legs, peel the skin up to where the grey scales of the foot begin and cut through the skin so that the entire leg is free and exposed. Next, roll the bird onto its side, grip the leg firmly and ease it back on itself until the ball-and-socket joint in the hip pops out, then use your knife to slice through the meat between the ball and socket and remove the leg. Repeat on the other side.

**5** You now have plenty of options. If using the legs for Bird Lollies (see page 102), we leave

the feet on. Otherwise, we snip off the legs with secateurs, pull out and discard the sinews and use the legs for a batch of confit (see technique on page 82) or for stews. If any of the breast is particularly well 'shot', you can remove any bloody, damaged tissue with a boning knife.

## How to tunnel bone

The main reason for tunnel boning is so you can stuff an entire bird and, once cooked, carve it perfectly across the grain of the meat (see Buckin' Duck, page 124). You can remove the wing, leg and thighbones completely, but we always leave them in, as they are some of the best bits to gnaw on. This technique is a lot easier than you may think. It involves removing the entire breastplate, ribs and backbone and is done using a combination of a small paring knife and your fingers.

Once you have your bird plucked, drawn and 'oven ready', place it breast-side up on a chopping board. Starting at the top end of the bird, where the neck was, gently pull back the skin and a bit of flesh to reveal the wishbone. Grasp firmly with a couple of fingers, and gradually pull it out until it is removed. Next, massage your fingers down the breastplate and around the ribs of the bird, gently teasing the meat off the bones with your fingers until you reach the other end of the bird.

The next step is to separate the legs and wings from the bird's body. Bend the legs back on themselves towards the back or spine side of the bird so that they pop out of the sockets. You may need to use the knife to separate any bits of cartilage or tendon.

The wings are a bit more fiddly, as is removing the spine. Flip the bird over so it is breast-side down then slide the knife under the skin from the neck end of the bird. Carefully separate the

spine from the skin, including the shoulder bone of the bird, employing the use of your fingers from time to time until you've reached the back end of the bird. Then spin the bird around and, using your knife, separate the pelvis from the skin and meat.

Finally, gently draw the entire bone structure out of the bird from either end, using your knife or fingers to separate any bits that may still be connected. Have a feel inside the deboned bird to check for any remnants of bone.

Once you have stuffed the bird, truss it up at each end with butcher's string. You may need to sew up the neck end using a large needle, but the legs can be trussed together (another reason not to debone them).

# Plucking and drawing

**1** With plucking, your main aim is to keep all of the skin intact. You only want to pluck the main body of the bird and legs because all appendages will be removed. The skin on the breasts is quite delicate, so work carefully and remove the feathers here 'with the grain', meaning pulling them out in the direction they flow down the bird. For the legs and back of the bird they can be plucked 'against the grain', by pulling them back on themselves. Try to remove every bit, even the under-developed feathers that poke through.

**2** Once the body of the bird has been plucked, including the legs, take a pair of secateurs and cut the wings off at the shoulder, right up against the side of the breast.

**3** Next, remove the legs and sinews from within the legs. Using the secateurs, following the line of the grey leg scales, snip just halfway through the leg to break it, then twist the leg around and around. This helps to draw out the strands of sinew. Then pull firmly while gripping the leg to remove the foot and tough strands of sinew and discard them.

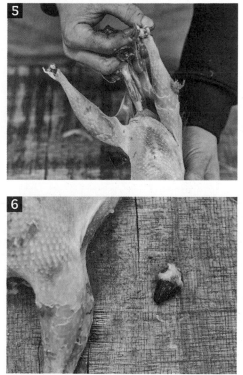

**4** We are now ready to 'draw' or gut the bird. Lay it on its back and, using a sharp knife, make a small incision just under the breastplate at the back end of the bird. Make sure you do this as lightly as possible – you just want to split the skin open, not the innards. You can then gently open the cavity up with your fingers.

**5** To remove the innards, slide four of your fingers into the bird, keeping nice and tight against the breastplate until your fingers reach far up inside to the neck end or top end of the bird. In a slow scooping action, draw out all of the insides, including the heart, lungs and trachea. Once this is removed, cut off the anus and the parson's nose (pope's nose) at the back end of the bird.

At this point, also make sure you have removed the crop (the alimentary tract where the bird stores food prior to digestion). This is found at the neck end between the wishbone and is likely to have some grain inside it from the bird's last meal.

**6** If the bird has been hanging for no more than a couple of days, it is worth keeping the heart and liver. They are tasty morsels. Check the bird for any feathers you may have missed. If necessary, you can use a blowtorch or a gas ring to do this for the finer stuff. Finally, give the bird a good clean and rinse inside and out before using.

# BUTTERMILK PHEASY BURGER

If you're ever looking for a way to convince a game sceptic of the virtues of pheasant, then this is your knight in shining armour. This recipe also appeals to children because it presents the pheasant in a way that is familiar to them.

*Serves 2*

# Ingredients

2 pheasant breasts
250ml/9fl oz/1 cup plus 2 tbsp
    buttermilk
500ml/18fl oz/2½ cups
    vegetable oil, for deep frying
6 tbsp plain flour (all-purpose
    flour)
1 tsp salt
1 tsp cayenne pepper

1 tsp smoked paprika

## To serve

2 brioche burger buns (brioche
    rolls or hamburger rolls)
6 tbsp Smoke-roasted Wild
    Garlic Mayo (see page 160),
    plus extra as desired
4 rashers of streaky bacon
    (slices of bacon)

2 slices of Monterey Jack cheese
mixed salad leaves or wild
    leaves
hot sauce of your choice

# Equipment

deep fryer (optional)
digital thermometer
blowtorch (optional)

---

One thing that we do like to do with both pheasant and partridge is to showcase how they can be used in untraditional ways and be treated in the same manner as chicken. This burger definitely gives its less wild cousin a run for its money.

# Method

Put the pheasant breasts in a bowl, pour the buttermilk over them, then cover the bowl and put it in the fridge for 1–2 hours or preferably overnight.

Just before cooking the pheasant is a good time to get the remaining components ready for your burger: fry the bacon in a hot pan and set it aside, then toast your brioche buns.

Heat the oil in a medium saucepan over a medium heat. Take extra care if you are doing this over a fire – a deep-fat fryer or gas ring may be preferable. You will need to get the oil up to 170°C/325°F.

While your oil is heating up, put the flour, salt, cayenne pepper and smoked paprika in a bowl and mix well. Remove each pheasant breast from the buttermilk, allowing any excess buttermilk to drip off before dropping the breast into your seasoned flour mix. Coat well and gently place the breasts in the hot oil. Fry for 1–2 minutes until golden. Once done, remove from the oil and drain on paper towels.

To assemble your burger, spread the garlic mayo on the top and bottom bun, add the burger and top it with the bacon, cheese, salad leaves and hot sauce. To melt the cheese, put the buttermilk burgers on a metal tray, lay on the cheese and take the blowtorch to it. Alternatively, grill them under a hot grill for 1–2 minutes until the cheese melts. Hot sauce is a matter of debate, and is really down to personal preference.

*TIP*
*Buttermilk is a great help with game. The lactic acid it contains helps to tenderize the meat. You see a similar approach in Indian cuisine, with the use of yogurt-based marinades. If you can, try to soak the pheasant breasts in buttermilk overnight, but 1–2 hours will suffice.*

# BLOWTORCHED PHEASY WITH ROSTI & BUTTERMILK SAUCE

Cooking any kind of meat with a blowtorch might seem strange at first, but 'torchin' is actually a very good way to cook with a serious degree of control, crisping the meat, rendering down fat and still being able to ensure a nice rare middle in the case of red meat.

*Serves 4*

# Ingredients

4 pheasant breasts, each cut
into 6 similar-sized pieces
4 tbsp pork fat, preferably
Iberico
leaves from 2 thyme sprigs
salt and freshly ground
black pepper
4 tbsp Bourbon Bacon Jam
(see page 167), to serve

a small handful of vetch and
crow's garlic, to garnish

## For the Ground Ivy Rosti

450g/1lb waxy potatoes,
peeled and grated
1 handful of ground ivy,
finely chopped
4 tbsp melted butter

2 tbsp goose fat or vegetable oil,
for frying

## For the Buttermilk Sauce

200ml/7fl oz/scant 1 cup
buttermilk
juice of 1 lemon

## Equipment

blowtorch

---

The aim in this recipe is to achieve perfectly
cooked, moist pheasant, which is why this
method works so well: it gives you maximum
control with very little margin for error. It's
wonderfully satisfying to put together and the
result has incredible layers of taste and texture.

# Method

To make the ground ivy rosti, put the grated
potatoes in the centre of a clean dish towel,
gather up all four corners of the dish towel and,
holding the towel over the sink, twist the corners
together to squeeze as much moisture out of the
potatoes as possible. Twist and squeeze until the
potatoes are dry, then transfer them to a bowl.
Add the ground ivy and butter and season with
salt and pepper, then mix thoroughly.

Using your hands, shape the mixture into four
equal-sized balls and then, on your palm, flatten
each one out into a 1cm (½in) thick cake, making
sure each rosti is tightly pressed together.

Heat a large frying pan over a medium-high heat
and add the goose fat. When it is hot, add the rostis
and fry for 4–5 minutes on each side until golden
brown and crisp. Remove from the pan and drain
on a paper towel, then set aside in a warm place.

To cook the pheasant, put the pork fat in a
saucepan and heat it over a medium heat until
melted and clear, then remove from the heat.
Add half of the thyme leaves, taking care because
they will spit and crackle as they infuse into the
fat. Set the pan aside.

While the fat cools a little, make the buttermilk
sauce. Put the buttermilk and lemon juice in
a small saucepan and season with salt, then
set aside until ready to warm it through just
before serving.

Season the pheasant pieces with a little salt,
put them in the warm, melted fat and roll them
around to coat. Then, using a blowtorch, cook the
pheasant very gently for 3–4 minutes, moving
the flame back and forth over the pheasant and
shaking the pan to roll the pieces over. You are
looking to just brown the edges of the meat.
When the meat is well browned, cover the pan
with foil and leave it to rest for 1–2 minutes.

Warm the buttermilk sauce over a medium heat
for 1–2 minutes, then put a spoonful of the sauce
into each of the bowls. Top with the rosti, followed
by a couple of dollops of the bacon jam, then
arrange the pheasant on top. Sprinkle with the
vetch, crow's garlic and remaining thyme leaves.

# WHOLE ROAST PHEASANT WITH HASSELBACK POTATOES

When it comes to selecting a pheasant to roast, always go with henbirds, which are much more tender than cockbirds. Earlier in the season is best when the birds are young. The hardest thing about roasting whole pheasant is avoiding the dreaded dryness and ensuring the bird is cooked through, so always use a good-quality fat for basting.

*Serves 2*

## Ingredients

1 whole pheasant, oven-ready
1 lemon, coarsely chopped
2 sprigs of thyme
2 garlic cloves, peeled and
    coarsely chopped
4 tbsp pork fat (preferably
    Iberico) or goose fat
salt and freshly ground
    black pepper

roasted vegetables and sauteed
    broccoli or kale, to serve
gravy, to serve

### For the Hasselback Potatoes

6–8 salad potatoes
    (waxy potatoes)
50g/1¾oz/scant ¼ cup butter
1 tbsp pork fat (preferably

Iberico) or goose fat
2 garlic cloves, peeled
    and finely chopped
leaves from 2 sprigs
    of rosemary
truffle (optional)

## Equipment

digital thermometer

---

**We accompany most of our roasts with hasselback potatoes. This fancy version of the humble spud was created in Sweden in 1953 by trainee chef Leif Elisson at Restaurant Hasselbacken. The technique is a bit fiddly, but well worth the effort.**

## Method

To make the potatoes, get your clay oven fired up (see page 31) or preheat your conventional oven to 220°C/425°F/gas mark 7. Put one of the potatoes on a chopping board and lay the handles of two long wooden spoons along the long sides of the potato to help prevent you from slicing all the way through. Working from one end of the potato to the other, make a series of cuts through the top of the potato, leaving about 3mm (⅛in) between slices and cutting downwards. Use the wooden spoons as a guide to make sure you don't cut all the way through. Repeat with the remaining potatoes, then put them in a baking dish, sliced tops up.

Melt the butter and pork fat in a warm pan, then spoon or brush the mixture over each potato and season well with salt and pepper. Sprinkle the garlic and rosemary leaves over the potatoes,

followed by a generous grating of truffle, if using. Bake in the clay oven for 1½ hours or in the preheated oven for 1 hour, basting occasionally.

While the potatoes are baking, prepare the pheasant. Stuff the lemon, thyme and garlic into the cavity of the bird and spread 3 tablespoons of the pork fat over the entire bird to coat well, then season with salt and pepper.

Heat a cast-iron pan over a medium heat and add the remaining 1 tablespoon of the fat. Once melted, put the pheasant in the pan on its back and cook for a few minutes until browned, then turn it onto its side and continue cooking and turning until browned all over.

About 20 minutes before the potatoes are done cooking, transfer the pheasant to the oven. Reduce the heat to 180°C/350°F/gas mark 4 and bake for 25 minutes until the pheasant is cooked through and has reached an internal temperature of 55°C/131°F and the potatoes are tender in the middle and crispy on top. Remove from the oven, wrap the bird in foil and leave to rest for 10 minutes in a warm place so that the internal temperature reaches 65°C/149°F. Serve with the potatoes and any other roasted veg.

# PARTRIDGE BIRD LOLLIES WITH FIRE-ROASTED PEPPER RELISH

*Serves 4*

## Ingredients

8 partridge legs, skinned, cleaned and
    completely feather-free
250ml/9oz/1 cup plus 2 tsp buttermilk
150g/5½oz/2 heaping cups panko
    breadcrumbs
1 tsp salt
1 tsp cayenne pepper
700ml/24fl oz/3 cups vegetable oil,
    for deep frying
1 recipe quantity Wild Salad (see page
    158), to serve

### For the Celeriac Remoulade

2 tbsp mayonnaise
1 tbsp Dijon mustard
juice of 1 lemon
½ celeriac, peeled and coarsely grated
    or finely sliced
1 tsp nigella seeds (black onion seeds)
salt and freshly ground black pepper

### For the Fire-roasted Pepper Relish

1 red onion
2 red peppers
1–2 red chillies
1 tbsp apple cider vinegar
1 tbsp olive oil
1 tsp granulated sugar
salt

## Equipment

rubber band
deep fryer (optional)
digital thermometer

These bird lollies started out as a canapé that we served with martinis at the end of our courses. We left the feet on so we could hang one on the edge of each glass. They proved such a hit that we decided to turn them into an appetizer and it remains one of the most popular dishes we've ever done at the Treehouse.

The key factor is to select only birds that have unbroken, fully intact legs. This recipe also works really well with pheasant legs; you'll just need to up some of the ingredients because they're slightly bigger. We still leave the feet on. They give you something to pick your teeth with afterwards. Classy.

## Method

Gather up all the partridge legs in a bunch with the feet at the top and fasten them together, using a rubber band, to create a 'bouquet'. Pour the buttermilk into a bowl and put the meaty ends of the legs into it, keeping the feet sticking out. Put them in the fridge for 1–2 hours or preferably overnight. The acid content in the buttermilk will help to tenderize the legs.

We cook a lot of our meat and veg 'dirty' or directly on the hot coals (see page 34). You can do the pepper relish in the oven but it won't have the same smokiness or charred flavour. Once you have a good bed of hot coals, fan off any ash from the coals so they are really glowing. Put the onion directly on first, as it will need the longest. After 5 minutes, add the peppers and then add the chillies. Keep an eye on them and cook for 20–30 minutes, turning them every so often until charred all over and softened. Remove from the heat, transfer to a plate and leave to cool.

Once cooled, brush the vegetables off lightly by hand – not too much because those charred bits will add colour and flavour. Next, deseed the peppers then either

chop everything finely by hand or pulse a few times in a blender. Transfer to a bowl and mix in the vinegar, oil and sugar and season with salt. You can serve it cold or warm it gently in a saucepan.

To make the celeriac remoulade put the mayonnaise, mustard and lemon juice in a bowl, season with salt and pepper and mix well. Stir in the celeriac, then cover and chill in the fridge for at least 20 minutes and up to 24 hours before serving. Sprinkle with the nigella seeds when ready to serve.

When ready to cook the partridge legs, heat the oil in a medium saucepan over a medium heat. Take extra care if you are doing this over a fire. A deep-fat fryer or gas ring may be preferable. You will need to get the oil up to 170°C/325°F.

While the oil is heating, put the breadcrumbs, salt and cayenne pepper in a bowl and mix well. Pull out each leg from the buttermilk, letting any excess buttermilk drip off, then coat the leg well in the breadcrumbs.

Completely immerse the legs, feet and all in the hot oil in pairs and fry for 1–2 minutes or until lightly golden, then remove and drain on paper towels. These are best served immediately, but you can also cover them with foil and keep them warm in the oven at 100°C/200°F/gas mark ½ for a short time, just be careful they don't dry out. Serve with the pepper relish, celeriac remoulade and wild salad.

**TIP**
*You can make pepper relish well in advance when you have a fire on the go. It will last for up to 2 weeks if stored in the fridge. Feel free to play around with other veg and don't be afraid to add more chillies for extra heat.*

# SPATCHCOCKED MISO PARTRIDGE WITH ASIAN SLAW

This is the ultimate recipe for grilling partridge straight over hot coals. Partridge is a delicate bird that doesn't need much time at all over a hot bed of charcoal, so spatchcocking gives us the advantage of just two cooking surfaces to deal with.

Whether you want to hit the birds with a barbecue rub, go buffalo-wing style or put together a marinade of any kind, this is definitely one of my favourite ways to cook them. The Asian slaw adds a fresh contrast to the spicy, smoky, umami-rich partridge. It's also great with pheasant and pigeon.

## Method

In a bowl, mix together all of the ingredients for the marinade and set aside.

To spatchcock the partridge, put it breast-side down on a chopping board and, using a pair of secateurs or kitchen scissors, start at the back end of it and cut up through each side of the spine and remove the entire backbone. Then, open up the bird with your hands and splay out the ribcage so you flatten the bird out. Repeat with the other bird.

*Continued on page 107*

*Serves 2*

## Ingredients

2 partridges, plucked and drawn
vegetable oil, for oiling the grill

### For the marinade

2 tbsp of red miso paste
2 tbsp vegetable oil
1 tbsp sesame oil
2 tbsp honey
1 thumb-sized piece of ginger root, peeled and very finely grated
1 garlic clove, peeled and very finely grated
1 tbsp mirin
1 tbsp soy sauce
juice of 1 lime
1 tbsp rice wine vinegar
½ red chilli, finely chopped

### For the Asian Slaw

1 daikon, peeled and coarsely grated
1 carrot, peeled and finely sliced
1 handful of coriander (cilantro) leaves, chopped
1 small handful of three-cornered leek or wild garlic (ramps), chopped
1 small handful of yarrow
1 tsp fish sauce
juice of ½ lime
1 tbsp rice wine vinegar
salt

## Equipment

baster
digital thermometer
2 skewers (see box on page 107)

Add both partridges to the marinade, massaging it well into both birds. Cover the bowl and pop it in the fridge to marinate for 30 minutes to 1 hour or, ideally, overnight.

To make the Asian slaw put the daikon, carrot, coriander leaves, three-cornered leek and yarrow in a bowl and mix together. Add the fish sauce, lime juice and rice wine vinegar and toss well. Season with salt and set aside.

When you're ready to grill the partridges, get your fire going. Position the grill nice and low over the coals so that you are working over a high heat. Remove the partridges from the marinade and set the marinade aside; you'll need it for basting once the grilling begins.

Oil the grill to prevent the meat from sticking to it, then mount the birds on skewers, put them on the grill breast-side up and grill for about 10 minutes. Then flip them over and baste with some of the remaining marinade, using a baster or brush. Grill for a further 5 minutes and then flip and baste the breasts once more. This is not so much about timings, but it is all about temperature. Using a digital thermometer, check the breast and legs. You are looking for an even 55°C/131°F before the birds are ready to pull off. You want a nice bit of char and a sticky golden surface on them. Wrap in foil and rest for 5 minutes, then serve with the Asian slaw.

**TIP**

*If your carrots come with their leafy green tops, chop up a handful of these herbaceous leaves and add them to the slaw when you add the coriander.*

## WHITTLE YOUR OWN SKEWERS

Skewer selection is always a matter of debate. Any skewer will live up to the job, but if you happen to be in the woods with no skewers to hand, cut down a few thin bits of hazel. You often find them growing up straight off the main branches of the tree. Ideally they need to be about 1cm (½in) thick and definitely 'green', meaning alive and full of moisture so they won't burn on the grill. Get your whittling hat on and cut them to your desired length before shaving the bark off with a knife, leaving a few inches on at the bottom to serve as a handle.

# GOCHUJANG PARTRIDGE KEBABS

This Korean dish really illustrates the versatility of game and how there is no need to stick to the traditional when the quality of the meat is able to hold its own. Most game birds, especially partridge, respond very well when paired with Asian ingredients. The mild gaminess pairs beautifully with spice, heat and citrus. This recipe also works great with venison. Cooking with fire adds a wisp of smoke to the proceedings as well.

*Serves 2*

## Ingredients

1 tbsp gochujang paste

zest and juice from 1 lime

1 tbsp sesame oil

2 tbsp finely chopped coriander
    (cilantro) stems

4 partridge breasts

vegetable oil, for oiling the grill

2 corn tortillas

1 recipe quantity Asian Slaw
    (optional; see page 105)

a small handful of coriander
    (cilantro) leaves

1 tsp sesame seeds

1 lime, cut into wedges, to serve

salt

## Equipment

digital thermometer

2 skewers (see box on page 107)

---

So, what is gochujang? It's a sweet, spicy, savoury paste made from chilli powder, fermented soya beans (soy beans) and glutinous rice with a little sweetener added. It's wonderfully punchy, so use it sparingly. You can buy it in some Asian supermarkets or online. Once you've tried it, you will have one of those 'where have you been all my life' moments. Just try not to put it on everything.

## Method

In a bowl, mix together the gochujang paste, lime zest and juice, sesame oil and coriander stems. Mix well and then add your partridge breasts, making sure they are well covered in the marinade. Cover the bowl and pop it in the fridge. If you can marinate these overnight, you will be happy you did, but 30 minutes to 1 hour will suffice.

When you're ready to cook, get your fire going. Take the partridge breasts out of the marinade and weave two of them onto each skewer, piercing at the bottom end of the breast and then sliding the skewer through the top of the breast. Once you have a good bed of hot embers to grill over, brush some of the oil over the grill

to prevent the meat from sticking to it. Put the skewers on the grill and season with salt. Grill for 3–4 minutes on each side. Unlike chicken, partridge can be served pink so we can retain its delicate moisture. Cooking over fire is less about timings and more about temperature. When your digital thermometer hits 55°C/131°F when probing the partridge, it's done.

To serve, briefly toast the tortillas on the grill. Slide the breasts off the skewers and onto the tortillas. Top with the slaw, if using, and sprinkle with the coriander leaves and sesame seeds. Serve with the lime wedges for squeezing over the top.

*TIP*
*This recipe also works really well with the Smoke-roasted Wild Garlic Mayo on page 160 or the slaw used in the Dirty Doe Tacos on page 66.*

*"Wood pigeons have an insanely good diet, thanks to their penchant for a diverse range of farm crops as well as for foraged foods..."*

# WOOD PIGEON

**Of all the birds we shoot for the pot, if there is one that really stands high above the others it is the humble wood pigeon. If steak could fly, it would be a wood pigeon. If you wanted a formidable test of your skill with a shotgun, then this bird will give it to you and probably hand your ass to you on a plate. They're awesome, both in the field and in the kitchen.**

**B**EFORE GOING ANY FURTHER, let's be clear: these are not the same dodgy-looking birds found pecking around central London. Those feral pigeons are definitely not fit for eating. Wood pigeons are the very prolific country version that, more often than not, find themselves on the bad side of local farmers because of the serious damage they do to newly sown spring crops, such as oilseed rape (canola), peas, beans, mustard and maize (corn). Fortunately, there's an app for that and it's called decoying.

Decoying lets you shoot large numbers of 'woodies'. I've only been to a couple of 'proper' driven shoots over the years, but none has been quite as testing as a day on the decoys. It involves building a hide on the edge of a field where the pigeons are regularly feeding on a certain crop and then setting out a series of fake wood pigeons to lure in others. While sitting in the hide, you shoot the birds as they come in. There is quite a bit more to it than that, but that's the general gist of it.

Wood pigeons are well equipped when it comes to survival. They have amazing eyesight and are very nimble on the wing too, able to clock up some serious speed, especially with a tailwind. This makes them quite a challenge to take down. They are also fairly bulletproof, and are able to emit a puff of feathers from what would be seen as a direct hit and keep flying. Wood pigeons have

an insanely good diet, thanks to their penchant for a diverse range of farm crops as well as for foraged foods, such as clover leaves, berries and even whole acorns in autumn. You can tell if a wood pigeon has been eating acorns because it will drop like a ton of bricks when you shoot it, and leave a small crater in the ground. Naturally, these birds are going to taste amazing.

Typically, the breasts or the whole 'crown' (both breasts on the bone) are the most sought-after cuts. The best way to cook it is to sear the breasts in a hot pan skin-side down for a couple of minutes on each side and then rest for 7–8 minutes in a warm place. It is imperative that it is served pink, and a disaster if it is overcooked. When you add in the element of smoke to proceedings... wow.

Wood pigeon can also be roasted whole and the legs are very good slow-cooked or given the confit treatment (see page 82). The carcass makes for a fine stock, too. To deconstruct a wood pigeon, follow the butchery guide on page 92.

There really is so much to love about the wood pigeon: there is a challenge to it; they are the most free-range bird in the UK; there is no closed season and no horrific price tag attached to shooting them... and when they land in your kitchen, they really impress with a rich, red meat that is more akin to fillet steak in texture and flavour. It's that good.

# WOOD PIGEON CARPACCIO

*Serves 4*

## Ingredients

6 skinless pigeon breasts
1 lemon, cut into wedges

### For the marinade

150ml/5fl oz/scant ⅔ cup olive oil
4 tsp apple cider vinegar
1 small bunch of wild garlic (ramps),
    coarsely chopped, or 2 garlic cloves,
    peeled and coarsely chopped
1 carrot, peeled and coarsely chopped
1 stick of celery, coarsely chopped
1 small red onion, peeled and
    coarsely chopped
1 tsp salt, plus extra for seasoning
2 sprigs of rosemary
4 bay leaves
freshly ground black pepper

### For the carpaccio accompaniments

wild horseradish, grated
1 handful of young horseradish leaves,
    rocket (arugula) or watercress
5–6 sprigs of vetch
a small handful of Jack-by-the-hedge
10 sorrel leaves
40g/1½oz/½ cup grated or shaved
    Parmesan cheese
1 tbsp chopped gherkins
1 tbsp capers, drained
1 tbsp olive oil
crusty bread

A lean red meat, wood pigeon is perfect for carpaccio. We've found that an overnight marinade with some veg and herbs really elevates the final dish and helps to work as a bit of a cure.

Carpaccio is a rather recent taste sensation from the 1950s. It's attributed to Giuseppe Cipriani, the owner at the time of the famous Harry's Bar in Venice, Italy (Harry's Bar was also the home of the Bellini). Carpaccio was born when a customer by the name of Countess Mocenigo informed Cipriani that her doctor had recommended she only eat raw meat. The colours of the final dish reminded him of the paintings by the Venetian painter Vittore Carpaccio, so Cipriani named it after him. Now we've all learned a little something, let's cook... or not, in this case.

## Method

In a large bowl, mix together all of the ingredients for the marinade and season with black pepper. Add the pigeon breasts, making sure they are covered by the marinade. Cover the bowl and chill in the fridge for at least 12 hours or, ideally, overnight.

Remove the breasts from the marinade, put them on a freezer-proof plate and freeze for 45 minutes before constructing the final dish, so you can slice them wafer thin.

When ready to serve, slice the pigeon breasts as thinly as possible. Arrange them on a large serving plate with all of the accompaniments and squeeze the lemon wedges over the top. Season with salt and pepper and serve with crusty bread. Great with a fine red wine.

# HOT-SMOKED PIGEON CROWNS

Pigeon crowns are both breasts still on the bone. They are able to stand up to a bit more cooking, which is why they are perfect for hot smoking. For this recipe, you really want to be using a proper hot smoker or a conventional kettle-style barbecue. The important factor is maintaining a cooking temperature of 100–125°C/200–250°F. With traditional kettle barbecues, you will need to have a drip tray filled with water for the pigeon crowns to sit over.

*Serves 4*

# Ingredients

4 pigeon crowns
1 tbsp olive oil, plus extra
    for basting
1 red onion, peeled and
    finely sliced
1 red cabbage, finely sliced
1 tsp caraway seeds
20 asparagus spears
1 tbsp butter
juice of 1 lemon
salt and freshly ground
    black pepper

# Equipment

kettle-style barbecue with drip
    tray or a hot smoker
a few chunks of cherrywood
    or applewood
digital thermometer

---

To prepare the pigeon crowns, pluck the breast portion of the bird and then make an incision, as if you were going to draw or gut the bird (see page 94). Holding the bird in your hand with the head end closest to you, put two fingers underneath the breastplate through the incision and pull firmly towards you as if opening a hinge and the whole crown should come away from the bird. Wash well and they are ready to go.

# Method

Put the coals on one side of the barbecue to produce an indirect heat. Fill the drip tray with water and put it in place, then light the barbecue and adjust the vents underneath so they are half closed.

Baste the pigeon crowns with the oil and season with salt and pepper. When the barbecue has reached a temperature between 100–120°C/200–250°F, put the pigeon crowns, breast-side up, over the drip tray. Add a few chunks of cherrywood or applewood to give them a good hit of fruity smoke from the start, close the lid and keep it closed to avoid losing temperature very quickly.

Cook for 30 minutes, then check for doneness, using a digital thermometer. Once they reach 50°C/131°F, you can give them a quick blast over

direct heat, using tongs, to get a bit of a sear on the skin, then remove them from the heat, wrap in foil and leave to rest for 8 minutes.

While the pigeon crowns are resting, bring a pan of water to the boil and heat a frying pan over a high heat. Add the oil to the frying pan, then add the red onion, cabbage and caraway seeds and cook, stirring occasionally, for 6–8 minutes until the onion and cabbage are tender. Transfer to a serving bowl and set aside.

When the water is boiling, add the asparagus and cook for 1 minute, then drain and transfer to a bowl cover. Add the butter and lemon juice and season with salt and pepper. Toss well, then put the asparagus spears directly on the grill for 2–3 minutes to give them some colour.

Unwrap the pigeon crowns and serve with the cabbage and asparagus.

*TIP*
*Give this dish even more flavour*
*by adding chopped onions, herbs*
*and a little red wine vinegar to*
*the water in the drip tray.*

# DIRTY PIGEON BREASTS WITH PEAS & WILD GREENS

With some wonderful wild greens working through it, this dish delivers a hit of spring. Peas are one of the pigeon's favourite snacks and are a perfect complement to the bird. They're also one of the many crops we shoot them over with decoys. Seems ever so fitting.

## Method

Get a really good bed of charcoal on the go; cherrywood works very well with pigeon. When it is ready, fan off the ash, season the pigeon breasts with salt and put them directly on the red-hot embers, skin-side down. Cook for 2–3 minutes on each side, then wrap in foil and leave to rest next to the fire for 7–8 minutes.

Meanwhile, bring a saucepan of water to the boil, add the peas and cook, covered, over a medium-low heat for 2 minutes, then drain. While the peas are cooking, heat a frying pan and add the butter, then add the hogweed buds and cook for 1 minute. They will suck up the butter, so add a little more, if necessary. Stir in the peas and mint leaves and season well with salt and pepper. Cook for a further 1 minute, then remove from the heat.

Unwrap the pigeon breasts and slice them in half through each breast at a slight angle. Serve with the peas and sprinkled with the vetch and three-cornered leek flowers.

*Serves 4*

## Ingredients

4 pigeon breasts, skin on
350g/12oz/2½ heaping cups
    frozen peas
2 tbsp butter, plus extra, if needed
12 hogweed buds
leaves from a few sprigs of wild mint,
    coarsely chopped
12 vetch tops
a few three-cornered leek flowers
salt and freshly ground black pepper

NO TRESPASSING

VIOLATORS
WILL BE SHOT

SURVIVORS
WILL BE SHOT
AGAIN

"Considered a red meat, duck also presents the luxury of being able to serve it rare, while rendering in its own delicious fat."

# DUCK

The duck or, specifically, the mallard, as it is known in the world of quarry species, is incredibly common in the UK and many other places around the world. Virtually any pond, river or lake will have its own population of this attractive, tasty waterfowl. In our neck of the woods, in the south of England, the duck season runs from the beginning of October to the end of January, and as long as until mid-February along the coast. Check your local resources to find out when the season begins in your area.

**M**Y FIRST CLOSE ENCOUNTER with a mallard as a child was by complete mistake. While using a handline off a bridge, hoping to catch one of the greedy carp that regularly showed themselves, my piece of bread crust, with hook well embedded, drifted under the bridge and was taken by a handsome drake (male mallard). I struck and ended up with quite a surprise as the duck took off with my line in tow. Doing what any normal ten-year-old would do, I took the duck home in my backpack with the intention of removing the hook properly and allowing a bit of convalescence before releasing him back to where he came from. The duck was probably a bit bewildered, living in a greenhouse with a paddling pool for a few days, but he recovered and was duly released back under the bridge and I could add animal husbandry to my juvenile skillset.

It wasn't until a few years later that I really got to appreciate them as a bird for the table when I got into beating to help flush birds out of the undergrowth and the shoot I was on had a couple of ponds they used for duck drives. Being paid in game from my bramble bashing opened up a world of different meat, and duck was the first one I remember really having an appetite for. Mallards are significantly smaller than the farmed duck we are used to from the butcher's or the supermarket. However, they have a lot more flavour. Considered a red meat, duck also presents the luxury of being able to serve it rare, while rendering in its own delicious fat. Preparation of

duck is the same as pheasant (see page 94), with a couple of differences to note. Always pluck them because the skin and fat are key when cooking and help self-baste the meat and keep it moist during the cooking process. Unlike the other game birds, ducks have a rather annoying layer of down underneath the bulk of the feathers. This can be removed by gently rubbing the skin with your thumb and fingers or by giving them a very quick blast with a blowtorch to singe the down and then rub it off by hand.

Duck is fairly easy to get hold of. Most butchers and game dealers will have mallard during the game season, and if you get to know your local shoot, where you can get involved in the action, either as a beater or a gun, you will be furnished with some excellent duck throughout the season.

## DUCK ISLANDS

The chasseur, or hunter, of the Landes region of south-western France uses a cunning method to attract ducks. They construct 'islands' known as huttes or gabions, places plastic decoys on the water around them and attaches a cage to the side. Inside the cage are live decoys – birds that have been bred for their call. They call in passing ducks or geese and alert the hunter to incoming fowl. All the chasseur has to do is take up his gun, flip open the flaps in the roof of the gabions and fire away at the approaching birds. Genius.

# DUCK HAMS

Eating duck is, for me, very much a guilt-free experience. I spent half my childhood feeding them, so it's only fair for them to return the favour. This recipe is based on one I picked up while living in south-western France in the Landes forest. Out there, duck is king. Livers, hearts, legs, breasts and gizzards are what keep the region alive.

*Makes 2 duck hams*

# Ingredients

2 large duck breasts with skin
   and fat intact
100g/3½oz/scant ½ cup fine
   sea salt
2 tsp freshly ground black
   pepper
4 bay leaves, finely sliced

leaves from 3 sprigs of thyme
1 tbsp dried hogweed seeds
2 tbsp red wine vinegar,
   plus extra if needed to
   seal leftovers
1 recipe quantity Mustard
   Seed Caviar (see page 155),
   to serve

pickled hogweed buds and
   pickled rocket (arugula) roots
   (see page 168), to serve

# Equipment

butcher's string
muslin (cheesecloth)

---

**Hogweed seeds, with their aromatic, orangey flavour, work perfectly with the duck. Duck hams are a great way to preserve the glut that is inbound when the season kicks off and a perfect snack to take on a shoot.**

# Method

Score the fat on the duck breasts in a cross-hatch pattern, using a sharp knife and going just down to the flesh. Set aside.

In a bowl, mix together the salt, pepper, bay leaves, thyme and hogweed seeds and then rub this cure into both sides of the duck breasts so that they are completely covered. Put a few sheets of paper towel on a plate, put the duck breasts on top, then cover them with a few more sheets. Put them in the fridge to cure for 24 hours.

After curing, remove the duck breasts from the cure and rinse under a cold tap. Pat the duck dry with a paper towel. Put the red wine vinegar in a shallow dish and dip the flesh side of the breasts in for 20 seconds, then dry well with more paper towels.

Put the breasts, fat-side down, on a muslin and roll up in a tight cylinder, ensuring there are no air pockets. Tie them up nice and tight with butcher's string from end to end.

Hang the hams in a cool, dry place with plenty of air flow, such as a garage or woodshed, for 15 days. They will be done when they give slightly when pressed between thumb and forefinger.

The hams will last in the fridge for 3–4 weeks, although you will probably devour them in one sitting. To seal them once used, just dip the cut end in some red wine vinegar. We tend to serve them as a taster dish (pictured opposite) with mustard seed caviar, pickled hogweed buds and rocket roots. They also make an excellent addition to any charcuterie board.

# CHERRY-SMOKED DUCK BREAST SALAD

This dish is an awesome combination of all the flavour sensations. Chicory and dandelion give it a touch of bitterness; the cured elements provide saltiness; the sorrel and lemon lend a sour note; and the pomegranate imparts a sweetness. The cured egg yolks and the duck itself add a rich umami hit, too. The final flourish is what we like to refer to as the sixth flavour sensation, which our human brains are hardwired to since man first discovered fire: smoke.

*Serves 4 as an appetizer*

# Ingredients

2 duck breasts

2 heads of chicory,
   leaves separated

1 handful of rocket (arugula)

1–2 handfuls of wild leaves,
   such as hairy bittercress,
   dandelion, yarrow and sorrel

juice of ½ lemon

2 tbsp olive oil, plus extra
   for drizzling

2 slices of sourdough bread,
   cut into small cubes

1 tbsp butter

seeds from 1 pomegranate

1 Cured Egg Yolk (see page 159)

salt and freshly ground
   black pepper

## For the cure

1 tbsp Chinese five spice

3 tbsp coarse sea salt

3 tbsp granulated sugar

1 tbsp dried hogweed seeds

1 tsp coarsely ground
   black pepper

# Equipment

non-reactive plastic container

portable hot smoker

cherry sawdust

digital thermometer

---

For a job like this, we use a portable stovetop smoker, which can be used directly on the fire or your conventional stove.

It's important to note that, in this recipe, we're not looking to cook the duck breasts by hot smoking them. We merely want to impart a good smokiness to them before finishing them off in the pan.

# Method

Put all of the ingredients for the cure in a bowl and mix well. Put half of the cure in a non-reactive plastic container and put the duck breasts, skin-side up, on top. Cover the duck breasts completely with the remaining cure and put them somewhere cool for 20 minutes.

While the duck is in the cure, put the chicory, rocket and wild leaves in a bowl. Drizzle lightly with the lemon juice and 1 tablespoon of the oil and season with salt and pepper. Toss well.

Heat a pan over a medium heat and add 1 tablespoon of the oil. Add the bread cubes and fry, stirring frequently, for 4–5 minutes until golden, then drain on a paper towel. Set the pan aside.

Remove the duck breasts from the cure, rinse under cold water and pat dry with paper towels. They should be slightly firm to the touch.

Prepare the hot smoker by putting a thin layer of cherry sawdust on the base of the smoker, then place the smoker directly on top of the fire or stovetop. Once it starts to smoke, add the breasts and close the smoker. Smoke for a maximum of 5 minutes. Any longer than that and you risk them becoming slightly overpowering and acrid.

Reheat the pan you made the croutons in over a medium heat. Add the butter and, once it has melted, add the duck breasts, skin-side down. Cook for 10 minutes until the fat has rendered and the skin has started to crisp up nicely. Flip them once and cook until the duck breasts reach an internal temperature of 55°C/131°F for a nice pink centre. Remove them from the heat and leave to rest for 5 minutes before carving into slices.

To serve, divide the salad onto four plates and arrange the slices of duck breast on each plate. Sprinkle with the croutons and pomegranate seeds, and grate some of the cured egg yolk over the top. Drizzle with olive oil, sprinkle with black pepper and serve.

# BUCKIN' DUCK

This has to be, hands down, the greatest game dish I have ever had. Originally conceived when some of us were staying overnight at the Treehouse after an autumn course, we took stock of what we had left to put together for some supper: a few mallard, a mix of different wild mushrooms we had found that day, some cuts of fallow deer and our larder staples.

*Serves 2 as a main*
*or 4 as an appetizer*

# Ingredients

1 duck, plucked, drawn and
   deboned (see page 92)
½ venison fillet, fat flank or
   bullet cut (about 350g/12oz)
salt and freshly ground
   black pepper

## For the Mushroom Duxelle

4 tbsp butter

2 garlic cloves, peeled and
   finely chopped
1 shallot, peeled and
   finely chopped
400g/14oz wild mushrooms,
   such as winter chanterelles,
   girolles, ceps (porcini)
   and hedgehog fungi,
   finely chopped
leaves from 2 sprigs of thyme
4 tsp vermouth
juice of ½ lemon

## For the jus

12 morel mushrooms, ideally
   fresh, sliced in half if large
2 tbsp butter
175ml/scant 6fl oz/scant ¾ cup
   red wine
500ml/17 fl oz/generous 2 cups
   venison or beef stock

# Equipment

butcher's needle and string
digital thermometer

---

What followed next, in time-honoured tradition, was a jovial game of one-upmanship, fuelled by Malbec, and the buckin' duck was born. It's a bit like a venison wellington, but with the fillet wrapped in a deboned duck instead of pastry. This is a dish I hope you will try your hand at. Nothing worth doing ever comes easy.

# Method

Once your duck is plucked, drawn and 'oven ready' you will need to debone it or tunnel bone it (see page 93). To make the mushroom duxelle, heat a large frying pan over a medium heat. Add the butter, then the garlic and shallots and cook, stirring occasionally, for 8 minutes until softened. Add the mushrooms, thyme and vermouth and season with salt and pepper. The mushrooms will release some moisture as they cook, so simmer for 15–20 minutes, stirring occasionally, until most of the liquid has evaporated. Add the lemon juice and adjust any seasonings, then remove from the heat and set aside to cool.

Preheat your oven to at least 180°C/350°F/gas mark 4 or up to a maximum of 200°C/400°F/gas mark 6, or get your clay oven up and running

(see page 31). Put the duck, skin-side down, on a chopping board and spread the mushroom mixture all over the inside of the duck, then put the venison in the middle. Season with salt and pepper, then fold up the sides of the duck. Using a butcher's needle and string, sew up the duck from the neck to the back end, then truss the back legs together. If the duck has been tunnel boned, gently fill the inside with the duxelle and slide in the venison from the back end, then truss the legs. Put the duck on a baking tray and bake for 40 minutes to 1 hour. Once you hit an internal temperature of 55°C/131°F, remove the duck from the oven, wrap it in foil and leave it to rest for 10 minutes before serving.

To make the jus, add 1 tablespoon of butter to a pan on a medium heat. Once melted, add the mushrooms and cook, stirring occasionally, for 6–8 minutes until browned, then add the wine and continue cooking until the liquid is reduced by half. Add the stock and reduce by half again. Add the remaining tablespoon of butter and whisk until glossy and thick, then season with salt and pepper. Slice the duck in half to reveal the impressive interior and serve it immediately, smothered in the jus.

GATHER

"... never eat anything unless you're 100 per cent sure of what it is. As a wise man said, everything is edible once."

# WILD PLANTS

**We as a species have always been foragers. The word essentially means 'looking for stuff' and while it doesn't have to be geared towards our stomachs, in modern times the term has become synonymous with wild plants.**

AT HGC, OUR JOB IS TO EDUCATE people and help them to understand wild foods as an ingredient, taste them in a context and encourage people to go forth, seek and experiment. We certainly don't have all the answers when it comes to wild plants and how to use them. I don't think anyone does or ever will. Out of necessity, our Mesolithic ancestors had a much deeper understanding of them and before the introduction of farming, foraging was a key part of sustaining life.

My own education of wild plants has been through many books and a lot of time in the field gathering, identifying and experimenting. Occasionally, I have met a 'guru' who could teach me an extraordinary amount, and I am truly thankful to those who are willing to share what they know. Experimentation is the key to enlightenment. There will be failures along the way, but there will be heroic conquests, too. Just make sure to always follow the most important rule of all: never eat anything unless you're 100 per cent sure of what it is. As a wise man said, everything is edible once.

This plant directory is not intended as an identification guide, but rather as an index of some of the plants we use on a daily basis, subject to the seasons. The focus is on the 'terroir' that we operate in around HGC and how we get the best out of them. For identification purposes, I urge you to look at some of the great resources that are out there and then get at least three for cross-referencing. The key to learning about wild plants is in the actual structure of the plant from stem to leaf.

What makes the use of wild plants so enticing and enjoyable is that there is often only a short window of opportunity. These are not ingredients you can simply pick off a shelf and they are not a click away. You have to work for them, you have to plan for them, you have to take time for them.

Every great plate of food should have a story behind it, like the time you got stung to bits harvesting nettles for pesto or beer because you had forgotten your gloves. Or the time you fell out of a tree trying to get Douglas fir tips. These, my friends, are real food stories and ones that you will repeat every year with the same gusto as you did the year before. There is adventure in wild food and while discovery may perhaps be the end goal, the journey that got you that ingredient is always the bit that tastes the best.

*"That time that you stank of garlic for days after collecting vast swathes of wild garlic for lacto-fermenting and making pesto."*

# PLANT DIRECTORY

This plant directory is not intended as an identification guide, but rather as an index of some of the plants we use on a daily basis, subject to the seasons here in the UK. The focus is on the 'terroir' of the landscape we operate in and how that affects the plant's character, the tasting notes of the plant in particular and how we get the best out of them.

### Yarrow
*Achillea millefolium*

**SEASON** January–December

**FAMILY** Daisy

**FLAVOUR PROFILE** Herbaceous, aromatic and slightly bitter, with back notes of rosemary and subtle hints of cucumber.

**USES** Young leaves and flowers work well in salads; larger ones have a slightly unpleasant texture unless pan-fried very briefly. Infuses very well into vinegars and alcohol, and makes a good garnish for drinks and food. This is the other half of 'gruit' along with ground ivy, which was originally used to flavour beer.

**HARVESTING NOTES** Found almost everywhere. Try to harvest the younger leaves: they have a clustered white flower head in July, which makes them easier to spot among the grass.

### Ground elder
*Aegopodium podagraria*

**SEASON** April–August

**FAMILY** Carrot

**FLAVOUR PROFILE** Herbaceous, notes of celery, slightly aromatic and mild back notes of lemon.

**USES** Leaves tend to be slightly papery. Use young leaves raw in salads or as garnish, older ones are best cooked down for soups and stews in the same way as spinach. Works well as an infusion into vinegars, for lacto-fermentation and for wild cocktail infusions.

**HARVESTING NOTES** A legacy of the Romans and part of the carrot family. Very common in gardens – once it's in, you can't get rid of it. The leaves look very similar to elder, hence the name. Always aim to take young leaves, as they have a much better texture and are much more versatile.

### Jack-by-the-hedge
*Alliaria petiolata*

**SEASON** April–June

**FAMILY** Cabbage

**FLAVOUR PROFILE** Also known as garlic mustard, which perfectly describes its flavour, Jack-by-the-hedge is a member of the cabbage family. This is certainly evident on eating. It has slight notes of bitterness in the aftertaste.

**USES** Best used in its raw state. Great addition to salads, salsas and chimichurri-type sauces. The seed pods found in June are excellent for flavouring pickles and vinegars. The roots are like a miniature spicy parsnip and the flowers make for a fine garnish.

**HARVESTING NOTES** Often found on roadsides, verges or around hedgerows. Snip off the top of the plant or pull off individual leaves.

# Three-cornered leek
*Allium triquetrum*

**SEASON** January–May

**FAMILY** Lily

**FLAVOUR PROFILE** Not as punchy as wild garlic (ramps) and with much sweeter overtones. A mellow garlic/mild shallot flavour.

**USES** Best used raw. It's not great for cooking due to the structure of the plant; so if you are going to cook it, add at the last minute. Brilliant for lacto-fermentation, dehydrates well. The whole plant is edible and the flowers make for a tasty garnish.

**HARVESTING NOTES** Much more common than you might think. Quite often an urban dwelling plant and mistaken for 'whitebells'. Let your nose be your guide. It sometimes appears as early as December.

# Wild garlic/ramps
*Allium ursinum*

**SEASON** February–May

**FAMILY** Lily

**FLAVOUR PROFILE** Strong garlic flavour, almost slightly spicy. Best used sparingly as it can have a tendency to overpower other flavours.

**USES** Possibly the most versatile of all wild plants and one of the best known. Wild garlic (ramps) presents us with garlic flavour, but in a green leafy form. The entire plant is edible from root to flower. Excellent for lacto-fermentation; scapes (buds) are great for pickling or drying, flowers for garnish, seed heads for pickling, leaves for just about anything, including wrapping meat. The bulbs aren't as fierce as standard garlic but can be found all year round if you know where to look.

**HARVESTING NOTES** You will probably smell it before you see it. Often found growing in profusion, it will last into June if in a well-shaded woodland. This is a plant to watch carefully as there is a different part to harvest each month throughout its life cycle.

# Crow garlic
*Allium vineale*

**SEASON** December–June

**FAMILY** Lily

**FLAVOUR PROFILE** The garlic flavour sits somewhere between wild garlic (ramps) and three-cornered leek, with a hint of chive running through it.

**USES** Use just as you would chives. Also quite a good addition to add flavour to pickles and vinegars. Makes for an unusual but fancy garnish. The purplish flower heads are a good addition to salads.

**HARVESTING NOTES** Quite often overlooked. Keep an eye out for them on verges and borders growing in small clumps. If you see something resembling chives then it's worth smelling them. Clip off a few leaves with scissors or a knife from each plant.

# Burdock
*Arctium minus*

**SEASON** April–September

**FAMILY** Daisy

**FLAVOUR PROFILE** Leaves and stems are edible when young, but intensely bitter. The root is what you are after – like a fibrous potato in texture with a pleasant, earthy, nutty flavour.

**USES** We use the large leaves to wrap food in before placing in the embers, which is great for fish and meat. The root is the part you want to harvest. Once out of the ground, peel off the outer skin and finely slice the core, either in the round or lengthwise. We pickle these then grill them over hot coals – they are truly delicious. They respond particularly well to a Mexican rub or a Japanese-style dressing.

**HARVESTING NOTES** Challenging! It grows in hard, stony ground and takes some digging to get out. If you can find burdock on the edge of a ploughed field, minimal digging is required. I have found harvesting them in spring/early summer yields a good root, and in autumn, too.

# Horseradish
*Armoracia rusticana*

**SEASON** January–December

**FAMILY** Cabbage

**FLAVOUR PROFILE**
Unmistakably horseradish. The wild stuff is a lot more potent than the cultivated variety, with a wonderful earthy heat with hints of spice.

**USES** This is the king of all things venison. Freshly grated on carpaccios, lacto-fermented for a top-quality horseradish sauce, blended into crème fraîche for a milder version or smashed together with water pepper for a wasabi hit with fish. It infuses well into alcohol: we created a horseradish and ground ivy vodka that made for an epic Bloody Mary. Very good with smoked fish and red meat. The young leaves can be used in salads for a spicy hit.

**HARVESTING NOTES**
A member of the cabbage family. If you know where it grows, you have a year-round harvesting window for the roots. Harder to find in the winter: look for the very small heads of tiny, frizzy leaves. You will need a sturdy garden fork for harvesting as the gnarled roots go down deep. Don't worry about getting the whole root out as it is remarkably persistent and will come back immediately. Stick any root off-cuts straight back in the ground and you will have a fresh colony appear the following year. Processing can be challenging – sinigrin, the volatile oil in horseradish, is vicious. Wearing eye protection (goggles or a diving mask, for example) and working outside will help when grating it.

## Hairy bittercress
*Cardamine hirsuta*

**SEASON** January–December

**FAMILY** Cabbage

**FLAVOUR PROFILE** A cross between rocket and watercress, milder in flavour with a healthy dose of pepperiness.

**USES** There are more uses beyond the salad leaf and garnish for this one. It makes an incredible pesto: use with wild garlic (ramps), toasted hazelnuts, parmesan, olive oil and a little lemon juice and seasoning. Works very well as a sauce or dressing with meat and fish.

**HARVESTING NOTES** Being available all year round, there are very few places you won't find it. As a first colonizer on waste ground, it prefers damper, shadier areas; most flower beds will have it growing in them. It tends to grow in rosettes, so harvest the whole rosette and snip off the bottom. Keep with plenty of moisture once picked, as it has a habit of degrading quickly, especially if individual leaves are picked.

## Cuckoo flower/ lady's smock
*Cardamine pratensis*

**SEASON** April–June

**FAMILY** Cabbage

**FLAVOUR PROFILE** One of the most awesome flavours in the wild, the leaves sit somewhere between mustard, horseradish and wasabi, with slight notes of something vaguely medicinal. The white/pinkish flowers have the same flavour but in a milder form.

**USES** Works well with anything smoked or grilled. You only need to use a little bit because it is quite punchy. It pairs nicely with earthy flavours. Can work well in a salad if used sparingly, but this is the ultimate garnish plant for full-on flavour.

**HARVESTING NOTES** Often found in damp areas or around watercourses, it looks quite similar to hairy bittercress before it flowers because they are in the same family. The basal leaves are broader, but the ones on the stems are very good. The flowers can be used too. May is the prime time to spot them – look for the flower heads.

## Rosebay willowherb
*Chamerion angustifolium*

**SEASON** April–September

**FAMILY** Willowherb

**FLAVOUR PROFILE** Shoots and pith are fleshy and sweet in taste, like a mild version of asparagus; the bright pink flowers that appear in late summer also have a wonderful sweetness to them.

**USES** The young shoots, when up to 20cm (7in) tall and still fleshy, are great as an asparagus alternative. Simply blanch and grill or pan-fry with butter, seasoning and a squeeze of lemon juice. The flowers provide a garnish. When the seed heads come out in September, they are like small bursts of fine cotton wool and we use them as tinder to light our fires with

**HARVESTING NOTES** In early April, harvest the shoots; strip off the leaves, as they tend to be slightly bitter. July sees the tall spikes of rose-like flowers appear. This is a good time to remember where the patches of them are for harvesting spring shoots. In the USA this plant is known as 'fireweed' because it is often one of the first colonizers on burnt ground.

# Ground ivy
## Glechoma hederacea
**SEASON** January–December
**FAMILY** Mint
**FLAVOUR PROFILE** Very much an all-round herb with predominant flavours being reminiscent of sage and rosemary with back notes of mint and thyme. Smell is quite distinctive, very herbaceous.
**USES** Definitely one to cook with. Works very well with rabbit. Treat it as you would a sprig of rosemary, or combine with other ingredients in rubs and marinades. Makes for an excellent vinegar. Use the flowers for garnish.
**HARVESTING NOTES** Along with yarrow (see page 130), this was the other ingredient in gruit, which was originally used to flavour beer before hops. The leaves are shaped like a horse's hoof, hence its other name, 'ale hoof'. Pretty much found anywhere, in full sun it tends to look like the one pictured. In the shade it mats out a lot like ivy and has much larger leaves. Smell is the key to identification if in any doubt.

# Meadowsweet
## Filipendula ulmaria
**SEASON** April–August
**FAMILY** Rose
**FLAVOUR PROFILE** The leaves have notes of marzipan and watermelon. The stem is very medicinal, smelling strongly of antiseptic with slight back notes of cheap, cherry-flavoured sweets. The flower heads have a floral, delicate vanilla scent with hints of almond. Like elderflower, it has its own flavour.
**USES** Meadowsweet flower heads can be used in much the same way elderflower is and in my opinion it is much more interesting. It makes an amazing syrup for cocktails and desserts. The sweet fragrance is very intense so it works especially well as an infusion. The leaves can also be infused and make for a good herbal tea. Meadowsweet used to be known as 'meadsweet' because it was originally employed to flavour mead.
**HARVESTING NOTES** From a medicinal point of view, we owe this plant a lot. Meadowsweet has very high levels of salicylic acid, which was originally isolated in this plant and used to create aspirin. Definitely a good plant to use in drinks. The leaves are best stripped of the stalks, to remove any traces of antiseptic flavouring: same with the flower heads. You will quite often find meadowsweet in ditches, damp areas and near water. They grow in large troops and you'll probably smell the sweetness of them in the air before you see them.

# Hogweed
## *Heracleum sphondylium*

**SEASON** April–September

**FAMILY** Carrot

**FLAVOUR PROFILE** Herbaceous, sweet and slightly aromatic with back notes of celery. The seed heads that appear in late June have an incredibly aromatic, orange-like flavour to them.

**HARVESTING NOTES** The carrot family, of which hogweed is a member, contains some very poisonous plants such as hemlock water dropwort (*Oenanthe crocata*), so make sure you fully understand what this plant looks like before harvesting (they look very different). Be sure you are harvesting common hogweed and not giant hogweed (*H. mantegazzianum*). Again, there is a difference in mainly size and leaf shape, plus you are less likely to find giant hogweed in the wild in the same way you do with common hogweed. Always try to delve down to the base of the plant to reach the young leaves.

# Ox-eye daisy
## *Leucanthemum vulgare*

**SEASON** April–August

**FAMILY** Daisy

**FLAVOUR PROFILE** Leaves have a slightly aromatic flavour, with notes of cucumber and liquorice: very pleasant. Flower buds are slightly more intense. Petals have a lovely sweetness to them.

**USES** The leaves are an excellent addition to salads – again, this is a plant best used raw. The leaves also infuse well into alcohol, as do the flowers. The flower buds can be pickled like capers or lacto-fermented.

**HARVESTING NOTES** Unmistakable in summer and found in meadows, verges and waysides. Leaves are available for the duration of it being in season. Pick them straight off the stem. You will only have a short period to harvest the buds in May.

## Pineapple weed
### Matricaria discoidea

**SEASON** May–September

**FAMILY** Daisy

**FLAVOUR PROFILE** Closely related to chamomile, pineapple weed does what it says on the tin: there's an intense hit of pineapple, the aroma is strong, but the flavour is not as playful.

**USES** Definitely one to capture in spirits, infusions and desserts. Infuses well into cream and muddles beautifully into cocktails for a tropical touch, and makes a great syrup. It can be used as a salad leaf or garnish, too. The whole plant is edible.

**HARVESTING NOTES** A member of the daisy family and found mostly on scrubland, field verges or poking out of pavements on the edges of car parks, it thrives in the most unlikely of places. Use before they seed when the flavour tends to diminish. It looks a lot like chamomile but without white petals. Like wild garlic (ramps), you will probably smell it before you see it, especially on a hot summer's day.

## Water mint
### Mentha aquatica

**SEASON** April–September

**FAMILY** Mint

**FLAVOUR PROFILE** Strong mint flavour, a cross between peppermint and spearmint.

**USES** Use as you would any kind of mint. Flower heads make for an excellent garnish. Use in North African, Mediterranean or Asian-style dishes and in wild cocktails.

**HARVESTING NOTES** Often found in or around water, this is by far our most common mint. If in any doubt use your nose to help with identification. Just pick off the first few sets of leaves. Very easy to identify by the distinctive purple/pink flower heads when it flowers in late June.

## Wild marjoram
### Origanum vulgare

**SEASON** April–September

**FAMILY** Mint

**FLAVOUR PROFILE** Essentially a wild version of oregano, the flavour is the same but a little more raw and stronger than cultivated varieties.

**USES** Anywhere you would use oregano. The leaves are at their best in early June. We use them in our chimichurri for venison and lamb, also as one of many herbs tucked behind our oak-planked salmon. The flowers make for a fine garnish.

**HARVESTING NOTES** Often found in large clumps, it definitely favours higher ground, such as the South Downs in England. Well worth drying out for future use. Very easy to harvest by hand, just pinch off the first few sets of leaves. If in any doubt, use your nose – the smell is unmistakable.

# Wood sorrel

*Oxalis acetosella*

**SEASON** April–December

**FAMILY** Wood sorrel

**FLAVOUR PROFILE** A stronger citrus hit than common sorrel, wood sorrel packs a good punch and with less of the apple-peel flavour. Much higher levels of oxalic acid so use sparingly.

**USES** Best used raw, as it doesn't cook well due to its delicate structure. The leaves make an excellent garnish and work particularly well with fungi and red meats, especially pigeon. The flowers are also edible.

**HARVESTING NOTES** Often found in vast carpets in deciduous woodland, the unmistakable clover-like leaves are a bit awkward to pick. Definitely a job for scissors: try to ensure that you leave as much of the stalk as possible behind because they uproot easily.

# Water pepper/arsemart

*Persicaria hydropiper*

**SEASON** May–September

**FAMILY** Dock

**FLAVOUR PROFILE** Hot. Very hot. Kind of like chilli heat, but not. After 10 seconds of chewing, a searing heat gradually dissipates. Not unpleasant, but certainly needs doctoring due to a slight medicinal edge to it.

**USES** This plant gives us wild heat. Anywhere you would look to use chillies, this is the plant. Bashed together with wild horseradish, it makes for an excellent wasabi hit. It infuses well into alcohol for Bloody Marys and adds a nice hit to salsas and slaws. Leaves and seeds are both edible: seeds make for a good seasoning.

**HARVESTING NOTES** Not to be confused with pale persicaria (*Persicaria lapathifolia*), which has black chevrons on the leaves and tastes of nothing. You will often see it near water or in damp areas in the middle of a wood.

# Primrose

*Primula vulgaris*

**SEASON** March–May

**FAMILY** Primrose

**FLAVOUR PROFILE** The pretty yellow flowers that appear in spring have a great sweetness to them with honey-like notes. The leaves, while good when young, become quite bitter when larger.

**USES** Flowers excellent for syrups, puddings, adding colour and sweet notes to wild salads. Young leaves can be used raw or cooked.

**HARVESTING NOTES** Often found on banks and along the hedgerow in spring, primroses are synonymous with Easter when they are in full flourish. Try to pick only a few leaves and flowers from each plant.

## Damson
### *Prunus domestica*

**SEASON** September–October
**FAMILY** Rose
**FLAVOUR PROFILE** Plum-like in both flavour and texture. Some variants may be slightly more tart than others.
**USES** Treat them as you would any other plum. High in pectin, so perfect for jams and jellies. Good for pickling and fermenting: they make the best umeboshi (Japanese pickled plum). Great for sauces with any kind of game and especially good for damson gin, made in the same way as you would sloe gin. Very interesting in a whisky, too. The blossom, like many members of the rose family, gives syrups a nice almondy/marzipan flavour.
**HARVESTING NOTES** Very easy to pick as the tree doesn't get especially tall.

## Sloe/blackthorn
### *Prunus spinosa*

**SEASON** October–November
**FAMILY** Rose
**FLAVOUR PROFILE** Extremely tart and acidic, quite astringent and with the ability to dry out your mouth when unripe.
**USES** Sloe gin. They also make very good jellies, jams and syrups, and can be brined and pickled similar to damsons.
**HARVESTING NOTES** Sloes are found in almost every hedgerow in the UK. Always pick straight after the first frost (or in October when they have ripened you can stick them in the freezer overnight): this breaks down the cell structure of the sloe so it will give out its juice a lot more easily. Watch out for the blackthorns – they have bacteria on them that will feel like a bruise the next day if you are pricked. You can tell the difference between a sloe and a damson as sloes have thorns and damsons don't.

## Douglas fir
### *Pseudotsuga menziesii*

**SEASON** January–December
**FAMILY** Conifer
**FLAVOUR PROFILE** Heavy citrus notes of grapefruit, lemon zest; subtle hints of spice and pine.
**USES** Just the needles. Works very well infused into alcohol for a martini and makes a fine syrup for cocktails and desserts. Also makes a very good vinegar. We often cook venison with it: pile plenty of sprigs straight on hot coals and then drop various cuts of meat on top for a gentle bit of smoke.
**HARVESTING NOTES** Do not confuse with yew (*Taxus baccata*), which is poisonous. To the untrained eye they can look similar – Douglas fir is more Christmas tree-like in appearance and a lot taller. The needles are around all year, but ideally you want the light green tips in spring. Use a pair of secateurs to snip off what you need and be prepared to do some climbing if there are no lower branches within reach.

## Stag's horn sumac
### *Rhus typhina*
**SEASON** August–September

**FAMILY** Cashew

**FLAVOUR PROFILE** Tart, lemony and slightly zesty. This is the spice known as sumac.

**USES** To make the spice, dehydrate the freshly picked clusters of claret-coloured berries or buds overnight, then rub them through a sieve or fine mesh so a rough powder comes out. You now have the spice sumac, used in Turkish and North African food. Perfect with all veg and meat, it is also used in cocktails. Place the buds in a jug of water and leave for a day in the sun, strain, then add a little sugar for a lemonade or 'sumacade': mixed with pineapple weed and rum, it makes an awesome concoction.

**HARVESTING NOTES** This is a common garden/ornamental plant. Be wary of any other sumac that doesn't have red 'stag horns'. Harvest in September when the claret colour is vibrant. Give them a squeeze, they should have a little 'give'. Snip off the buds at the base with secateurs.

## Dog rose
### *Rosa canina*
**SEASON** August–January

**FAMILY** Rose

**FLAVOUR PROFILE** Tart, super-citrusy with undertones of subtle sweetness.

**USES** This makes the best syrup for cocktails and desserts, and has a fairly long season to be harvested in. The flowers make for a great syrup too, but the best part is in the hips themselves. Super-rich in Vitamin C, the syrup is incredible in cocktails and can be drizzled over dessert or on ice cream. For savoury dishes it is a little like pomegranate molasses in the way it can be used.

**HARVESTING NOTES** Again, like sloes, can be found in most hedgerows. Flowers in May and fruits from September onwards. For syrup making, make sure you have a really good sieve AND muslin (cheesecloth): the hairs that sit around the seeds are an irritant and you want to make sure you get rid of them all. Once they are slightly soft in December, that's the time to pick them.

## Bramble
### *Rubus fruticosus*
**SEASON** August–September

**FAMILY** Rose

**FLAVOUR PROFILE** Blackberry. Varying from sweet and juicy to slightly tart, a good size is often an indicator of sweetness. There are over 400 micro species of blackberry in the UK, all with different levels of flavour.

**USES** Use as you would any other juicy berry – in jams, syrups, sauces, cordials, desserts... Pickling or fermenting the green berries works well and the young leaves in spring make for a fruity beer when brewed. The first shoots that appear on the plant in March taste similar to macadamia nuts and are best used raw. Blackberries work well with pigeon, duck and venison.

**HARVESTING NOTES** In early to mid-August, the berries at the tip of the bramble will be the sweetest and juiciest, the rest will ripen as the season goes on and all will vary slightly. Traditionally, you shouldn't pick any after 29 September, as apparently the devil urinates on them then.

# Sorrel
## *Rumex acetosa*

**SEASON** January–December

**FAMILY** Dock

**FLAVOUR PROFILE** A distinct lemony/citrus flavour with notes of apple-peel tartness due to the oxalic acid in the plant.

**USES** Lends itself to be used with fish, but also cuts well through red meat. Good as a salad leaf. Best used raw as it loses a lot of flavour and discolours when heated. Lemon zest helps to lift the citrus notes. The pink/green seeds make for a fine garnish, too.

**HARVESTING NOTES** A member of the dock family, sorrel has an obvious shield-shaped leaf, often found on verges and in open fields. A good way to spot it in June is by the seed heads, which form visible rusty-coloured clusters above everything else. The basal leaves (the cluster at the base of the stem) are the ones to pick, and spring is the best time to harvest young leaves. Also keep an eye out for sheep's sorrel (*R. acetosella*), which has more of a flared shield shape to it.

# Elder
## *Sambucus nigra*

**SEASON** May (flowers) August (berries)

**FAMILY** Honeysuckle

**FLAVOUR PROFILE** The flowers are uniquely floral, sweet and fragrant – very much a flavour of its own. The berries are juicy with a berry-like flavour and slightly sharp to taste.

**USES** Flowers: champagne, cordials, syrups, vinegars, infused directly into alcohol, desserts and even elderflower fritters. Few plants have been used in so many ways as this one. Berries: make a very good syrup, excellent for jam (often used as a bulking fruit for hedgerow jams); also make a very good sauce called Pontack, which is like a precursor to Worcestershire sauce, and similar in taste.

**HARVESTING NOTES** For the flower heads, harvest on a hot sunny day when the pollen will be at its peak, as this is where most of the flavour is. If in doubt, give a flower head a shake and you should see a cloud of yellow dust appear. Never harvest in the rain because it will all be washed off. Be sure to remove all stalks before use. The berries are one of the easiest plants to forage in abundance. Cook before use because elder contains minute traces of cyanide. A few raw berries are fine to eat, but any heat through processing will break down the toxin and render it perfectly safe. Only take a few from each tree and leave plenty for the birds and the bees.

# Alexanders

*Smyrnium olusatrum*

**SEASON** April–July

**FAMILY** Carrot

**FLAVOUR PROFILE** Intense, celery-like, of which this was a precursor. Very aromatic and floral.

**USES** Leaves and young shoots lacto-ferment well. The stems are good as a vegetable when peeled, then blanched or steamed – they are a lot milder in flavour. The seed heads once turned black are a great spice for food and as a botanical for gin or flavouring alcohol. Vodka is a good one to start with (the stems work for this, too).

**HARVESTING NOTES**

Alexanders are a member of the carrot family and flourish in coastal areas. Spring is an ideal time for harvesting stems: try to make sure they have a good flex in them as they can become a bit woody, so go for the tops. A knife or shears is best for this job. Either harvest seed heads when they are green/yellow for fresh infusions or wait till they turn black in June or July for long-term storage and use in food.

# Dandelion

*Taraxacum officinale*

**SEASON** February–November

**FAMILY** Daisy

**FLAVOUR PROFILE** A fresh green flavour with bitter notes to it. Flowers have a slight sweetness to them.

**USES** Incredibly versatile: the whole plant is usable. The roots are bigger than you might think and are a good source of carbohydrates. They can be pickled (see HGC Pickling Liquid, page 168) with a little soy added and then pan-fried for Asian style dishes, or cooked in bacon fat. The leaves are slightly bitter but make for an excellent salad leaf, the smaller the better: dressed with a little salt, sugar, oil and vinegar, they balance out nicely. The buds are great for lacto-fermenting and pickling to make a 'dandelion caper'. The flowers can be infused into alcohol, torn up and used as a garnish, turned into a very good country wine or made into a great syrup for cocktails and desserts. The stamens can be used as a poor man's substitute for saffron.

**HARVESTING NOTES** The first wild plant I ever harvested as a child. This plant tends to be available for most of the year, typically flowering in abundance in April/May. You would have to try pretty hard not to find it. Easy to locate because of the flowers in most verges and lawns, a small trowel will help to dig up the roots. Think of it as a wild version of chicory (endive) when using it – there is a similar flavour of bitterness to it. Smaller leaves are less bitter, but the bigger ones are still very good. Definitely a favourite of mine.

## Gorse
### Ulex europaeus
**SEASON** January–December
**FAMILY** Pea
**FLAVOUR PROFILE** The bright yellow flower heads have a slight coconut aroma to them and hints of sweetness.
**USES** Makes a great garnish for both savoury and sweet dishes. They can be used to make syrups for cocktails and added to lacto-ferments and pickles.
**HARVESTING NOTES** Quite an unpleasant one to harvest due to the spikiness of gorse. It's best to use a pair of secateurs to snip off the tops of the flowering limbs and process back in the kitchen.

## Nettle
### Urtica dioica
**SEASON** February–May
**FAMILY** Nettle
**FLAVOUR PROFILE** 'Nettle' is the best way to describe it because it has its own unique, very fresh and green flavour.
**USES** A versatile plant. In the kitchen, treat it like spinach. It requires blanching and will reduce down a lot after a few minutes in boiling water. You can use it raw if you toss it through flames, which will burn off all the tiny hairs that pack the sting. Use to make tempura, soups, pesto and in pickling. Also amazing in drinks, such as nettle beer, and it macerates well in alcohol, giving off a pinkish tinge – add sugar and you have yourself something that uncannily resembles a peach iced tea.
**HARVESTING NOTES** Pick only the first few sets of leaves or 'tops', ideally in the spring, but look for 'second cuts', where they have been mown or strimmed and pop up again. A sturdy pair of gloves is recommended for harvesting.

## Common vetch
### Vicia sativa
**SEASON** April–July
**FAMILY** Pea
**FLAVOUR PROFILE** Distinctly pea-like, fairly sweet and pleasant. Exactly what you would expect from a member of the pea family.
**USES** Flowers and leaves are the most useful parts. Use raw in salads, or they look stunning as a garnish. The small pea pods that develop are not particularly good for you unless they have been boiled for 2 hours, drained and washed first.
**HARVESTING NOTES** Just pick the top shoots of the plant, which will be the best for eating. May is when they flower and are at their prime; as you get in to June, they tend to become a bit woody and lose a lot of their pea-like flavour.

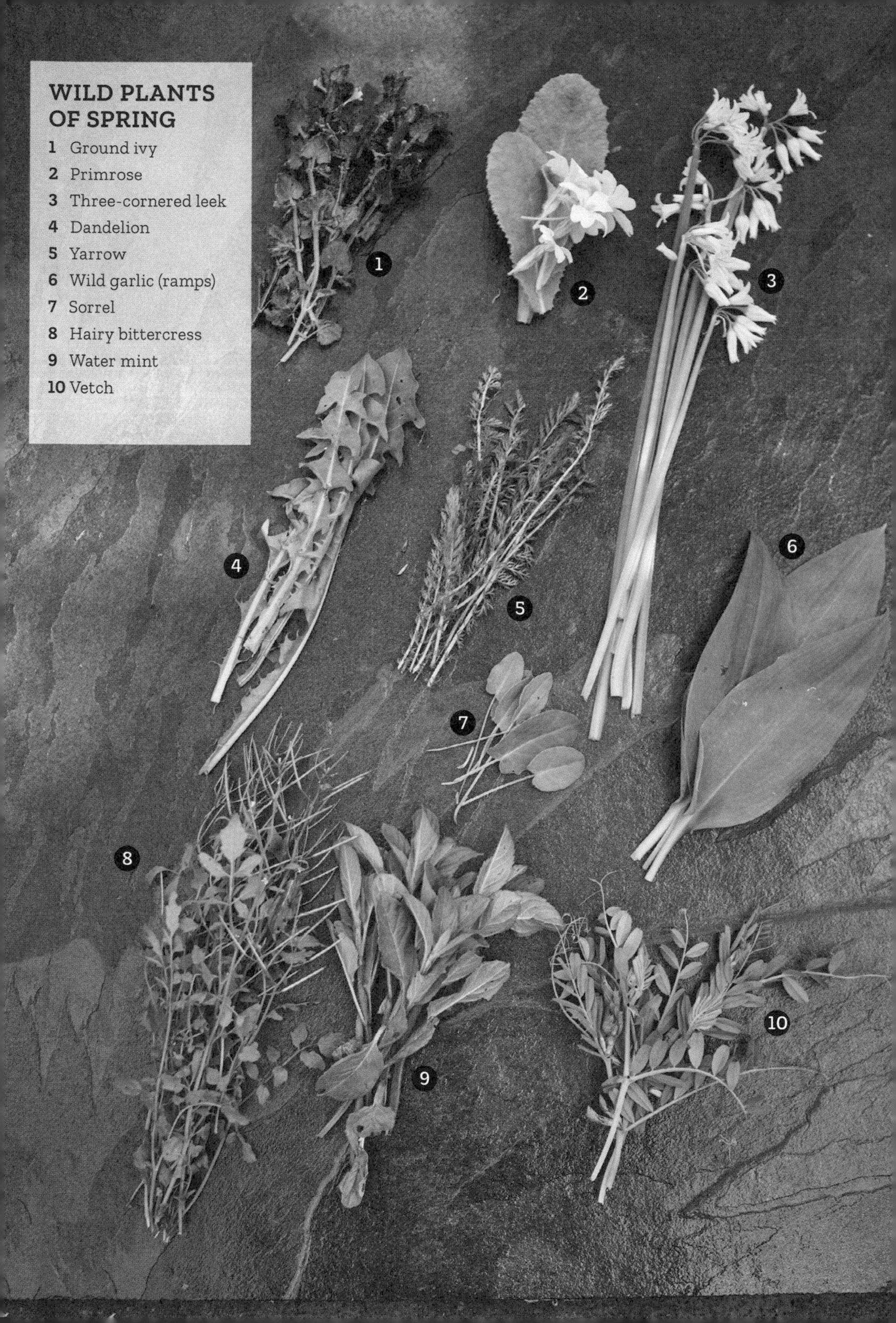


**WILD PLANTS OF SPRING**

1 Ground ivy
2 Primrose
3 Three-cornered leek
4 Dandelion
5 Yarrow
6 Wild garlic (ramps)
7 Sorrel
8 Hairy bittercress
9 Water mint
10 Vetch

# MUSHROOMS

**When it comes to wild food, mushrooms are an exciting part of the puzzle. There are some amazing edible mushrooms out there and only up to about 25 that are really worth eating.**

While it is imperative to have a healthy sense of caution when identifying wild mushrooms, the ones worth eating are quite easy to identify. That said, always be 100 per cent sure of your identification before even thinking about eating it. Experience in the field, reading, research, cross referencing and spore prints are all part of it. There is no fast-tracking when it come to this game.

Just like the Plant Directory on pages 130–143, this is not intended as an identification guide, merely an introduction to the fungi we use on a regular basis. There are books out there that go into serious detail on the subject, and I would urge you to get at least three for cross referencing if you want to get into your mushrooms.

With the selection we have here, just like the plants we use, it all comes down to 'terroir': this is what we have in our corner of the world and what we are most likely to find in the landscape we cook in. All of them are, with a bit of research and attention to detail, some of the easier species to identify. They are all excellent edibles and can be found at varying times of year.

## Field/meadow mushroom
### *Agaricus campestris*
**SEASON** June–October

**FLAVOUR AND TEXTURE PROFILE** Mild mushroom flavour and good texture, closely related to the button mushroom, but slightly more delicate.

**USES** A great mushroom for breakfast or on toast. Absorbs flavours very well. Excellent mushroom for duxelles and freezes well once cooked.

**HARVESTING NOTES** Often found on old pastureland, always in open fields and often in lines or rings. As a member of the Agaricus species, which contain some deadly mushrooms, be aware of the yellow stainer mushroom (*A. xanthodermus*), which looks similar and grows in the same places. Yellow stainers turn a vivid yellow straight after cutting and have a faint medicinal smell to them.

## Jelly ear
### *Auricularia auricula-judae*
**SEASON** January–December

**FLAVOUR AND TEXTURE PROFILE** Slightly unique, jelly-like texture, incredibly mild in flavour. Excellent flavour carrier.

**USES** This mushroom loves to absorb flavour in soups, stews and broths. Definitely NOT one for pan frying: it will spit a lot once in the pan.

**HARVESTING NOTES** A very popular mushroom in Asia. Almost always found on dead elder tree branches, it is an unmistakable mushroom and can be found all year round. Its other name 'Jew's ear' comes from a story that Judas Iscariot hung himself on an elder tree, and the mushrooms look like ears. Even when dried and shrivelled in the height of summer, just reconstitute in stock or boiling water.

## Bay bolete
*Boletus badius*

**SEASON** August–November

**FLAVOUR AND TEXTURE PROFILE** This is basically a slightly inferior version of a cep. It doesn't have the same level of sweet nuttiness, but is still good eating. The texture is good when young. Avoid picking in damp conditions, as it absorbs a lot of moisture and can be a bit slimy.

**USES** Exactly the same as a cep – it intensifies in flavour once dried.

**HARVESTING NOTES** These don't suffer from quite so much infestation as ceps, so even when larger specimens are found they are relatively maggot-free. Often found in deciduous and coniferous woodland, they are quite common. A good identifying feature is the pores, which when pressed bruise a bluish/green colour. They also have much slimmer stems. Try to pick firm young specimens.

## Cep/porcini
*Boletus edulis*

**SEASON** August–November

**FLAVOUR AND TEXTURE PROFILE** Excellent. The most highly prized of mushrooms. Sweet, nutty with a firm texture and the ability to be just as good raw as it is cooked.

**USES** Anything and everything. When sliced finely it makes for an amazing carpaccio with a light mustardy dressing, minuscule pieces of pan-fried pancetta and wood sorrel. Dries very well and dishes out big hits of umami on reconstitution: drying actually intensifies the flavour. Pickles really well, too. Pan-fried it is quite amazing with butter, garlic and thyme. You can't go wrong.

**HARVESTING NOTES** Unfortunately, this mushroom becomes infested by the larvae from fungal gnats, so it's best to pick when young but not too young – let it open up first to allow the spores to disperse. They are quick growers and often found in the light grass along the edges of woodland paths in mixed woodland. Also known as 'Penny bun' in the UK due to the baked appearance of the cap and its fat belly of a stem. Be aware of the bitter bolete (*Tylopilus felleus*), which has a paler cap and pinkish pores. Although not poisonous, it can ruin a plate of food with its intense bitterness.

## St. George's
*Calocybe gambosa*

**SEASON** April–May

**FLAVOUR AND TEXTURE PROFILE** Very firm textured mushroom with a great flavour.

**USES** Smells 'mealy' when fresh, which disappears when cooked. Incredibly versatile: works very well in stews, duxelles or compotes, but best when simply pan-fried with a little butter, garlic and thyme.

**HARVESTING NOTES** Found typically on or around St. George's day (23 April) but can appear in open pastureland in rings in April and May. The 'mealy' smell is a great indicator of identification and the fact that there are few other mushrooms you could mistake it for in spring is also helpful. Still a sense of caution is required, as it can look similar to the deadly fibrecap (*Inocybe erubescens*), which appears later in the year.

## Giant puffball
*Calvatia gigantea*

**SEASON** June–September

**FLAVOUR AND TEXTURE PROFILE** Good, white, fleshy, almost like a firm marshmallow texture. Fine mushroom flavour.

**USES** It can be cubed and pan-fried, cut into slices and pan-fried as a mushroom burger, or as a platform for further embellishment. It can also be hollowed out, stuffed and baked. It absorbs a lot of oil or butter when pan-fried and needs to be well seasoned.

**HARVESTING NOTES** The biggest one I've found was about 50cm (20in) in diameter. The best ones to harvest are anything the size of a football size or smaller, firm and white. As they get older they tend to yellow slightly inside: if there's any sign of this then don't use. Not something to actively search for – usually chanced upon and found on open grassland, often in good numbers.

## Chanterelle
*Cantharellus cibarius*

**SEASON** August–November

**FLAVOUR AND TEXTURE PROFILE** Amazing. Firm texture, incredible mushroom flavour that really holds and faint fruity notes as well as a slight pleasant earthiness.

**USES** Pretty much everything. They pan-fry well, although you may have to pour off some liquid to sear them a little: keep that liquid for stock. Can be eaten raw, in stews and in pies. They pickle exceptionally well.

**HARVESTING NOTES** Also known as girolle and often found in late summer. We find a lot on mossy banks in mixed deciduous woodland and under or around rhododendron too (also on banks). Try to avoid young specimens – give them a chance to get to a good size of around 3cm (1¼in) diameter. Be wary of the false chanterelle (*Hygrophoropsis aurantiaca*), which has a more iridescent orange colour to it rather than the lush apricot colour of the true chanterelle and often found with coniferous trees.

## Trumpet chanterelle
### Cantharellus tubaeformis

**SEASON** October–January

**FLAVOUR AND TEXTURE PROFILE** Quite a light-framed mushroom in terms of texture, but very good, solid, strong, earthy mushroom flavour with slight hints of fruitiness. Holds up to most forms of cooking.

**USES** Great for pickling or pan frying. Dehydrates readily and can be blitzed into a powder. Works very well when lightly dried or smoked in a wood-fired oven for about 10 minutes and served.

**HARVESTING NOTES** Some mushrooms have good camouflage. If you spot one, get down to their ground level and look closely – you may well find them carpeting the forest floor around you. Often found in and around pine or birch trees, hidden under bracken and occasionally in the open, they troop en masse in a good year. The yellow stem and greyish gills are true giveaways.

## Beefsteak
### Fistulina hepatica

**SEASON** August–October

**FLAVOUR AND TEXTURE PROFILE** Quite a full-on flavour, slightly acidic and tannic. Texture is good when sliced thin, not dissimilar to carpaccio (sadly not in taste).

**USES** Young specimens work really well when sliced finely across the grain, served raw and given a Japanese-style dressing of soy, mirin, ginger, spring onions, rice wine vinegar and chilli. Cooking does little for them: some suggest cooking in cream or soaking in milk but in my opinion it's not worth it. Let this one speak for itself.

**HARVESTING NOTES** Beefsteak are a bracket fungus found on oak and sweet chestnut trees. Pick only young specimens that are firm and exude some 'blood' when squeezed. You can really see where they get their name when you slice them in half: they have a marbling that Wagyu cattle would be jealous of.

## Velvet shank
### Flammulina velutipes

**SEASON** December–March

**FLAVOUR AND TEXTURE PROFILE** Unique flavour: mushroomy, distinctly sweet with notes of demerara. Good texture, slightly chewy.

**USES** Young specimens can be eaten raw, older ones best cooked. Works very well in stews, sauces and useful to use with late season game. Holds up well when pan-fried and retains its flavour. Works well in broths, phos and soups. It pickles quite well too, but retains a slightly slimy texture.

**HARVESTING NOTES** Almost always found on dead elm trees in clustered tiers and occasionally other deciduous trees. Abundant in January and February. Enokitake are a cultivated version of the same species, but grown in the dark. Be aware of the funeral bell (*Galerina marginata*) and the sulphur tuft (*Hypholoma fasciculare*), which look similar, but are usually long gone by the time the velvet shank appears. Just make sure it has a white spore print if in doubt.

## Hedgehog
### *Hydnum repandum*

**SEASON** September–November

**FLAVOUR AND TEXTURE PROFILE** For texture, it is one of the best of all the mushrooms. Firmness holds up really well when cooked; an excellent wild edible.

**USES** Best when pan-fried with a little butter. Due to its firmness throughout cooking, it works really well in pies, pasties, terrines and stews. Brilliant for pickling.

**HARVESTING NOTES** The ultimate 'fail-safe' mushroom. The creamy, slightly orange colour is unmistakable on the forest floor. Once you look at the underside you will see why: it has thousands of tiny spines instead of gills or pores. Only one other mushroom in the UK has them – the terracotta hedgehog, (*H. rufescens*), which is also edible. Often found in large numbers under beech and holly, but also other trees. Be sure to scrape off all the spines on picking, as they can get everywhere. This also helps disperse the spores in a place they already like to grow.

## Chicken-of-the-woods
### *Laetiporus sulphureus*

**SEASON** May–September

**FLAVOUR AND TEXTURE PROFILE** Chickeny in texture and to some degree flavour. It has a chicken/intense mushroom smell to it.

**USES** Holds up to all kinds of cooking. Often best blanched for a few minutes before use. Treat as you would chicken or tofu. It should always be well cooked before serving.

**HARVESTING NOTES** This picture shows the first one I ever found: quite a moment. Often found on oak trees, the bright orange/sulphur colour stands out clearly. Only harvest young specimens and leave anything old or chalky. Don't harvest from yew trees, as they can absorb toxins from the tree. WARNING. This mushroom can disagree with around 30 per cent of people, causing mild gastric upset. If you're trying it for the first time, only consume a small amount, which has been blanched and then well cooked, and wait for about an hour to see if it causes any issues.

## Parasol
### *Macrolepiota procera*

**SEASON** July–November

**FLAVOUR AND TEXTURE PROFILE** Very good, fine mushroom flavour. Texture when cooked is slightly soft and fibrous in a very pleasant way.

**USES** Stems are hollow and best for stock. The caps are the most useful and can be pan-fried or grilled whole or sliced when fully opened. Before they fully open they are at the 'drumstick' stage and perfect for stuffing and baking or for being battered and deep-fried. Makes a very good mushroom compote.

**HARVESTING NOTES** There is another parasol – the shaggy parasol – that can be edible, but disagrees with some people and lacks the good flavour of its cousins. True parasols have a distinctive stem with brown/black scales on them rather like snakeskin, which shaggy parasols don't have. Quite often found in large numbers in woodland clearings, open pastureland and occasionally in deciduous woodland.

## Oyster mushroom
### Pleurotus ostreatus
**SEASON** July–February

**FLAVOUR AND TEXTURE PROFILE** Excellent edible, quite a meaty mushroom in terms of texture. Flavour is delicate and can be mildly seafood-like in taste and aroma.

**USES** Excellent pan-fried or grilled, works very well in Asian-style dishes. This mushroom is familiar to many as it is cultivated quite widely.

**HARVESTING NOTES** Always found on deciduous trees, most notably beech, forming large clustered tiers. Ranging in colour from slightly blue/grey to beige. Cut them off at the base and be aware that older specimens can contain a few maggots. A good mushroom to find in winter. Do not pick anything from coniferous trees that looks like them because they could well be Angel wings (*Pleurocybella porrigens*), which are not edible.

## Scarlet elf cup
### Sarcoscypha coccinea
**SEASON** January–April

**FLAVOUR AND TEXTURE PROFILE** The texture may seem as if they might be a bit leathery, but it softens on cooking and holds its amazing colour. Flavour is good: earthy and mushroomy.

**USES** Good pan-fried and added to soups and stews.

**HARVESTING NOTES** One of the spore shooters. These are amazing fungi to observe. Every few minutes, what seem like small puffs of smoke pop out of them. These are spores shooting out. Often found in damp, mossy woodland with plenty of rotten trees. Unmistakable in early spring and hard to miss.

## Cauliflower fungus
### Sparassis crispa
**SEASON** September–November

**FLAVOUR AND TEXTURE PROFILE** Pleasant, earthy, nutty and mushroomy. Texture is good and holds up quite well to cooking, despite how it appears.

**USES** Very versatile. Takes a fair amount of preparation to clean properly of insects, earth and pine needles. Very good sliced and grilled like an actual cauliflower. Makes an amazing compote. Also dries very well.

**HARVESTING NOTES** Found at the base of pine trees and looks like a cauliflower. Often comes back around the same tree year after year and can grow to the size of a football. An amazing find. Be sure to leave part of it behind when harvesting.

# SIDES & BASICS

**Wild foods are so much more than fresh food at our fingertips. They all have distinct characteristic flavours and textures that can be enhanced in certain ways to really bring out the best in them, and sometimes even give them a complete transformation. If there's one thing that hedgerow foods benefit from, it's being pickled or preserved. Some of them are also quite suited to fermentation. But it's only through experimentation that we can really see what works. Occasionally, happy accidents happen and part of a plant you hadn't intended to use actually comes out much better (see Smoked Wild Garlic Salt, page 162).**

WHENEVER YOU VENTURE INTO the woods, fields and meadows as a gatherer, you revert to being feral: your senses are heightened and your eyes begin to separate the wheat from the chaff. Sorrel emerges: clover, meadowsweet and hogweed, too. For that moment the world turns quiet and the mental map of where such things are to be found kicks in. Of course, some things are meant to be found: with sustainable harvesting they come back every year and 'patches' are always going to be fruitful. Mushrooms on the other hand don't always play ball. Some species of fungi have better years than others, but they're always the ones that surprise you. Sometimes when you aren't looking for something, it will reveal itself.

We are incredibly lucky in this day and age to have so many wonderful herbs, spices and other ingredients from every corner of the globe, and to be able to combine wild flavours with these is a luxury indeed. There is such a thing as a 'fully foraged meal', but even that will need some basic larder ingredients to help it on its way.

Some of the recipes in the following pages draw from methods that are centuries old. Fermentation and pickling are nothing new to the human race: they were born out of necessity in order to preserve a glut that appeared for only a short window so they could be consumed and enjoyed at a later date. These days we are encouraged to eat with seasonality in mind,

which I wholeheartedly agree with, but if the larder can provide you with something harvested from a different season and preserved in some way it can add a whole new element to a dish.

Many of us are familiar with the five basic tastes: sweet, sour, bitter, salty and umami. These can be found in various wild ingredients and by preserving them in certain ways it can add new dimensions. Smoke is, as far as I'm concerned, the sixth taste, although this is perhaps considered more of a flavour component. The smell of smoke can trigger what's known as an atavistic or ancestral memory in our brains — we are hardwired to it. By involving smoke in the preparations of meat, vegetables or even the additional ingredients we use in a recipe, we can bring together the perfect mouthful. One thing that is always worth considering is the balance of a dish. While smoke is a wonderful thing, too much can be overpowering, so treat it carefully.

While the following recipes scratch the surface of what can be achieved when you master the techniques behind them, what we have here is a collection of our tried and tested favourites. Not all of them use wild ingredients, but what they can elevate other wild foods on the plate. The appetite for experimentation is a hungry monster that always needs feeding. One of the best ways to begin these experiments is to take a recipe you are familiar with and swap one of the ingredients for a wild ingredient and see what happens.

# VENISON STOCK

The foundation of any good kitchen is a fine stock, which can be used for all manner of different recipes and concoctions, such as the rich sticky jus for a Buckin' Duck (see page 124). We get through a lot of deer carcasses and we like to make the most of every single bit, from tanning the hides to using the bones for stock. Towards the end of a day of deer butchery at the Treehouse, we roast the bones over the embers of the fire, which gives the final stock a delicate smokiness.

*Makes about 1.5l/2½pt stock*

## Ingredients

1–2kg/2lb 3¼oz–4lb 6½oz venison bones and trim (any excess meaty bits)

1 tbsp rapeseed (canola) oil

2 onions, peeled

2 sticks celery

2 carrots, peeled and trimmed

2 parsnips, peeled and trimmed

4 garlic cloves, peeled

1 small bunch of ground ivy

2 sprigs rosemary

a few sprigs of thyme

6 juniper berries

125ml/4fl oz/½ cup red wine

1 tbsp salt

1 tbsp crushed black peppercorns

## Method

First, roast off the bones directly over hot coals on the grill or on a tray in the oven until they have a rich brown colour to them. Meanwhile, heat up a large stockpot and add the oil. Roughly chop all the vegetables, crush the garlic cloves and add them to the stockpot. Gently fry for 5 minutes until they have browned slightly. Add the roasted venison bones and trim, herbs, berries, wine, salt and pepper, then completely cover with cold water (about 2.25–2.8 litres/4–5 pints). Place the stockpot on a gentle heat and bring up to a gentle simmer. Try not to let it come to a full-on boil.

Simmer for 4–5 hours, using a ladle or large metal spoon to occasionally skim off any scum from the surface. Once ready, strain off the liquid and discard all the bones and vegetables. You can either freeze the stock for later use or reduce further for a richer stock. Be careful of adding any more salt, as this will intensify when the stock is reduced.

# MUSTARD SEED CAVIAR

If you're a fan of mustard, then this wonderful stuff
is definitely for you. When boiled, the mustard seeds
absorb the cooking liquid and pop in the mouth like
caviar. We use mustard seed caviar with a variety of
dishes. It works very well with charcuterie, rabbit,
venison and potato salads.

## Method

Put all of the ingredients and 125ml/4fl oz/½ cup water into
a saucepan and stir well. Bring to a rapid boil, then remove
from the heat and set aside to cool for 1 hour. Don't stir the
mixture, just leave the mustard seeds to absorb the liquid.

Return the pan to the heat and bring to the boil once again,
then remove from the heat and take out the bay leaves.
Pour the caviar into a preserving jar, tighten the lid and
leave to cool, then put it in the fridge for 3 days for the
flavour to develop before eating. It will keep in the fridge
for up to 4 months.

*Makes about 200g/7oz/1½ cups*

## Ingredients

100g/3½oz/scant ¾ cup yellow
    mustard seeds
350ml/12fl oz/1½ cups apple
    cider vinegar
4 bay leaves
2 tsp coarse sea salt
4 tbsp granulated sugar

## Equipment

medium preserving jar (about
    500ml/17fl oz/generous
    2-cup volume)

# CHARCOAL OIL

Flavoured oils are a great addition to your kitchen arsenal but they can carry the risk of food poisoning, most commonly when fresh produce is used to make them. Fresh produce has a good amount of water in it and when put in a low- or zero-oxygen environment (such as when submerged in oil), *Clostridium botulinum*, better known as botulism, can thrive. So to avoid any issue, always use oils infused with fresh ingredients within 24 hours. Use dried produce, such as dried herbs and dried chillies, for long-term flavouring. With charcoal, we have none of those risks because there aren't many things with less moisture content than charcoal.

rapeseed (canola). Olive oil works fine, but it has a touch more bitterness that comes through on the back notes. It's worth experimenting with different combinations. One fine match I stumbled upon was sesame oil and orange charcoal.

*Makes 400ml/14fl oz/1¾ cups*

## Ingredients

3–4 chunks of good-quality charcoal, burning
400ml/14fl oz/1¾ cups cold-pressed rapeseed oil
(canola oil), at room temperature

## Equipment

tongs
funnel
muslin (cheesecloth)
sterilized bottle, at least 400ml/14fl oz

Charcoal oil gives a smoky, barbecue flavouring to whatever you use it with. But there is such a thing as too much smoke in a dish. Balance is key. Different charcoals and wood that you have burnt down into charcoal all have slightly different flavours, so bear this in mind when you are going to make your oil. I find that fruitwoods make a very pleasant, lightly smoked oil. Apple, orange, plum and cherry are all excellent candidates. As the base, we tend to use a neutral oil, such as

## Method

This is an outdoor project and you'll need to get your coals going. Blowtorch or light the charcoal chunks until they are burning well. While your coals are getting ready, put the oil in a saucepan with a lid. Make sure the oil is at room temperature, or it will splatter when it comes into contact with the hot coals. When the coals are ready, blow on them to remove excess ash, then, using tongs, lift the coals and drop them into the pan of oil. Cover immediately with the lid to trap the smoke inside. Do not stir. It's the smoke that appears on contact with the oil that will make your infusion. After about 5 minutes, the charcoal will have given out its best and your infusion is done. Remove the lid, use the tongs to take out the charcoal and discard of it safely. Line a funnel with a muslin and put it in the sterilized bottle, then drain the oil into the bottle. Charcoal oil will keep for up to 4 weeks at room temperature; beyond that, the flavour doesn't hold as well, so don't be tempted to make a larger batch. Fresh and in small batches is best.

# BURNT ASH SALSA

Burnt Ash Salsa is a staple down at HGC. Also known as a salsa negra, because of the dark colour it takes on from dirty cooking all of the ingredients, it holds a rich smokiness and depth of flavour that is so incredible, you could just sit and eat it with a spoon.

## Ingredients

3 red onions
1 head of garlic
4 tomatoes
3 limes
2 red peppers
2 green peppers
2 red chilli peppers
1 small bunch of coriander leaves, finely chopped
1 tbsp olive oil
salt and freshly ground black pepper

## Equipment

tongs

The timing in this recipe is mostly down to the senses. You want your ingredients to be nicely charred, and they should be fairly soft to the touch. You can use this salsa with loads of recipes, including Rabbit Quesadillas (see page 84), Dirty Doe Tacos (see page 66) and Huevos Rancheros (see page 68). You can also use it as a condiment with beef or with any whole-animal cookery, such as a lamb. The key is to make sure you are using good-quality lumpwood charcoal (hardwood lump charcoal), or embers burnt down from logs. For more info on dirty cooking, see page 34.

## Method

Once you have a nice bed of charcoal or embers, give it a fan to remove any residual ash. Put the onions and garlic on first, laying them directly on the charcoal or embers, and cook them for about 10 minutes, turning every so often so they get a good char on them. Add the tomatoes, limes and red and green peppers to the other vegetables on the charcoal bed. These will take on colour quite quickly, so have a pair of tongs handy to flip them around as needed. Finally, add the chillies and keep a close eye on them because they cook quickly, in about 5–10 minutes, and can quite easily disappear and become part of the charcoal bed.

Once all the vegetables have a good bit of softness to them and are charred all over, take them off the charcoals, using the tongs, and give them a light dusting off with your hand. Put them on a metal baking tray, cover with plastic wrap and leave to steam and rest for 30 minutes.

Once rested, put the limes aside and deseed the peppers, including the chillies if you don't want your salsa too spicy. Reserve the chilli seeds so you can put some back in if you decide you want it spicier. Peel the onions and squeeze the garlic out of the cloves. Chop all of the vegetables and put them in a bowl. Add the coriander, then cut the charred limes in half and squeeze in the juice. Add the oil, mix well and season with salt and pepper, then serve.

# WILD SALAD

There is no better time of year than spring to construct a wild salad. The hedgerows are bursting with fresh, young leaves, foliage and flowers, which all have a variety of flavours that can add real character to salads. Of course, you can make wild salads throughout the year, it just may be more challenging come autumn and winter, but even then there are leaves available for use. Many of the flavours of wild greens may be new to you; others will be reminiscent of today's cultivated greens.

*Serves 4*

## Ingredients

4 handfuls of mixed seasonal wild leaves
3 tbsp olive oil
1 tbsp apple cider vinegar
½ tsp coarse sea salt
½ tsp sugar
¼ tsp freshly ground black pepper

Any combination of wild leaves work well. Some are more herbaceous than others, but you can even out the flavour by adding some conventional salad leaves and herbs. For the purists among you, going full-wild may be the only way. It will require a bit more work than your average salad but it will certainly taste better, will cost nothing more than time and will have been well nurtured by mother nature.

When making a salad like this, let the leaves do the talking and accent them only with a very simple dressing. This recipe follows the standard formula of three parts oil to one part acidity and is seasoned with a little sugar to add balance to some of the slightly more bitter wild leaves.

## Method

Put the wild leaves in a bowl and set aside.

In a small bowl, whisk together the oil, vinegar, salt, sugar and pepper until well combined. Drizzle the dressing over the wild leaves, toss gently and serve.

---

### WILD SALAD PLANTS

Here is the selection of plants that we use at HGC, all of which can be found in the Plant Directory (see page 130):

Cuckoo flower/Lady's smock
Dandelion
Ground elder
Hairy bittercress
Jack-by-the-hedge
Ox-eye daisy
Primrose
Sorrel
Three-cornered leek (wild leek)
Vetch
Wild garlic (ramps)
Yarrow

---

# CURED EGG YOLKS

Cured egg yolks are incredibly versatile. Try them finely grated over any kind of dish or use them to thicken salad dressings and sauces. You can also play around with all sorts of fresh herbs and different dried spices to flavour your yolks while they are in the cure.

## Ingredients

250g/8¾oz/¾ cup plus 1 tbsp fine sea salt
160g/5½oz/¾ cup plus 2 tsp granulated sugar
2 tbsp garlic granules (garlic powder)
6 bay leaves, finely chopped
6 eggs

## Equipment

plastic or non-reactive container,
     about 20 x 15 x 5cm/8 x 6 x 2in

## Method

In a non-reactive plastic container, mix together the salt, sugar, garlic granules and bay leaves. Transfer half of the cure to a bowl and set aside, then level out the cure remaining in the container so that it is about 1–2cm (½–¾in) deep. Using an uncracked egg, make six evenly-spaced depressions in the cure for the egg yolks to sit in.

Crack one of the eggs over a clean bowl and pour the contents into your hand. Jiggle the yolk between your fingers and let the egg white slip through into the bowl until you have a white-free yolk, then gently slip the yolk into the depression you made in the cure. Repeat with the remaining eggs.

Gently pour the other half of the cure over the egg yolks, covering them completely. Put the lid on the container and store in the fridge for 3 days.

After 3 days, take the yolks out of the container and rinse them gently under cold water to remove the cure, then gently pat them dry on a paper towel. They should be slightly translucent, firm to the touch and a wonderful golden colour.

To finish, preheat the oven to 100°C/200°F/gas mark ½ setting and line a baking tray with baking paper. Transfer the yolks to the baking tray and put them in the oven for 1½ hours or in a dehydrator for 2 hours. The cured yolks will keep for up to 3 weeks in the fridge in a sealed container.

TIP
*You can use the egg whites from this recipe to make meringues or freeze them for up to 12 months to use another time.*

# SMOKE-ROASTED WILD GARLIC MAYO

This mayo is a beautiful marriage of the cultivated and the wild, brought together by a hint of smoke. Smoke-roasting garlic is a slow process, so the garlic heads simply sit on the edge of the grill, where there will be enough smoke and heat to gently soften them over 4 hours. Similar results take just 2 hours in a clay oven (see page 31) or 2–3 hours in a kettle-style barbecue. You can also make this in a conventional oven but the result will lack the smokiness that really makes it special.

## Ingredients

1 head of garlic
1 small bunch of wild garlic (ramps) leaves, finely chopped
400ml/14fl oz/scant 1¾ cups mayonnaise
salt and freshly ground black pepper

## Equipment

pestle and mortar
medium-sized sterilized jar (about 455ml/ 16fl oz/2-cup volume)

Soft, caramelized, sweet and smoky, the garlic here partners perfectly with the punchy, no-holds-barred hit from the wild garlic to produce an irresistible mayo that money simply cannot buy. It goes very well with rabbit, hasselback potatoes and, quite frankly, everything.

## Method

Get your fire or barbecue going, or preheat a conventional oven to 200°C/400°F/gas mark 6. Put the garlic on the indirect side of the fire or barbecue or in the oven on a baking tray and leave it to roast. Check it every so often; it's done when it feels soft when you squeeze it. On the barbecue, the garlic should be ready in about 2–3 hours. In a conventional oven, it will take 30 minutes.

Once the garlic is done, pop each clove out of its skin, or break the head in half, put it in a saucepan, cover with the lid and shake vigorously for 30 seconds to magically peel the cloves. Put the cloves in a pestle and mortar and pound them into a paste, then spoon the paste into a mixing bowl.

Add the wild garlic and mayonnaise and season with salt and pepper. Mix well and adjust the seasoning, if necessary. Cover and store in the fridge for up to 3 weeks.

# BURNT ONION SALT

Seasoned salts, with their endless flavour combinations, are always worth experimenting with. As long as the ingredients you use are bone dry, you can smash anything together with salt to create your own signature seasoning.

## Ingredients

1 onion, trimmed, peeled and cut into quarters
coarse sea salt

## Equipment

kettle-style barbecue with a lid or clay oven
pestle and mortar
small jar

This one belongs to Chops, who made it for me in his first few weeks with us at HGC. It still gets used a lot and works particularly well with truffle chips straight out of the clay oven. It gives a lovely, roasted-onion finish to all manner of meat, fish or veg. Just use the best sea salt you can find because your final product will only be as good as the quality of the ingredients.

## Method

Get your clay oven fired up for this recipe (see page 31), then using your fingers, separate the layers of the onion and put them on a baking tray. Put it in the clay oven, then sit it at the mouth of the oven for 1–2 hours until the onion starts to blacken and crisp up, by which point it's ready. Just remove any bits that are still at all damp before continuing.

You can also cook the onion for 1 hour in a barbecue or in a conventional oven set at 120°C/250°F/gas mark ½ setting. Just make sure you are around to check on it because there's quite a difference in flavour between burnt and cremated.

To make the salt, pound a handful of the burnt onion and a little salt together in a pestle and mortar, adding more onion and a little more salt until you get the right flavour balance. It takes surprisingly little salt to get there. Store in a glass jar or plastic container for up to 1 year.

# SMOKED WILD GARLIC SALT

In spring, wild garlic is in full flow and by mid-April, this plant is ready to offer up its finest: just before the flowers appear, wild garlic buds or 'scapes' start to shoot up. You have a window of about a week to harvest, maybe a bit longer in well-shaded spots.

## Ingredients

400g/14oz wild garlic (ramps) scapes
coarse sea salt

## Equipment

barbecue with a lid
pestle and mortar
small jar

Scapes are amazing pickled, but you can't beat this flavoured salt for a knockout seasoning that pretty much works with any meat, fish or veg. It's a good idea to smoke a load of scapes and then make the salt as and when you need it. For reasons of sustainability, always make sure you are harvesting only a couple of scapes from each plant and ideally from a large, well-established patch.

## Method

The smokiness is a crucial part of this recipe's flavour profile, so fire up the barbecue for this one. Put some good-quality charcoal on one side of the barbecue and put the scapes in a deep baking tray on the other side so they can dry out indirectly, then put the lid on the barbecue and leave them to smoke for 2–3 hours.

Check the barbecue every 15 minutes. Try to keep it at around 190°C/375°F and jiggle the scapes around a bit. The aim is to get plenty of smoke into them as they dry out. When the scapes are completely dry and crumble in your fingers under the slightest pressure, you can store them in an airtight container for months.

To make the salt, pound a handful of the scapes and a little salt together in a pestle and mortar, adding more scapes and a little more salt until you get the right flavour balance. It takes surprisingly little salt to hit the sweet spot. Store in a glass jar or plastic container for up to 1 year.

# LACTO-FERMENTED WILD GARLIC

Lacto-fermentation may seem a touch daunting to begin with, but once you understand the basics, an entire new world of flavour and prospects begins to bubble away. Kimchi, sauerkraut, sriracha and yogurt are just a few of the lacto-fermented foods you may be familiar with, but the possibilities are endless. Most green stuff can be lacto-fermented, too, which is why it's such a great technique to add to the forager's arsenal.

*Makes 500g/17½oz/generous 2 cups*

## Ingredients

500g/17½oz/10 cups firmly packed wild garlic (ramps) leaves and stems, washed, dried and finely chopped
2 tsp fine sea salt

## Equipment

medium-sized preserving jar (about 500ml/17fl oz/generous 2-cup volume), sterilized

'Lacto' refers to *Lactobacillus*, bacteria that has the ability to convert lactose and other natural sugars into lactic acid, which inhibits the growth of harmful bacteria and preserves the product. Essentially, you use a small amount of salt to draw the liquid out of the ingredient once it's been chopped or sliced. The smaller you chop them, the more surface area there is for the salt to draw out moisture from. You then pound, scrunch and squeeze it so there is enough of its own liquid to submerge it in. It is then left in a warm place to let fermentation begin. The result is a tangy, punchy preserve that transforms and develops over time. Other than tasting awesome, these foods are also rich in probiotics, which are good for your gut.

## Method

Put a handful of the wild garlic in a bowl and sprinkle it with a bit of the salt. Repeat with another layer of wild garlic and salt and continue layering until all of the ingredients are in the bowl. Give it a thorough scrunch and stir with your hand, then set aside to rest for 30 minutes.

After 30 minutes, the salt will have started doing its job and now it's your turn. Get your hands in there and work it, squeezing as much liquid as you can out of the wild garlic and into the bowl. Transfer the wild garlic into the preserving jar and pour the liquid you've squeezed out over it. Then, using a spoon, pack the wild garlic tightly into the jar to ensure it is fully submerged and there are no air bubbles. You can use a stone to weigh it down and keep it submerged. Just make sure it is clean.

Seal the jar and leave it somewhere warm, ideally 24°C/75°F, to start the fermentation process. You will need to burp it every day by popping the lid. After about 7–10 days it should be ready, but you can always let it develop until you get the flavour profile you want. In the fridge it will be quite happy for up to 6 months.

# PROPER HORSERADISH SAUCE

Many versions of this classic sauce exist, but over the years it has been diluted and tampered with. This is the real stuff: a bacterial fermentation that mellows out a touch and even has a sweet edge, but still holds fire.

*Makes about 200g/7oz/1½ cups*

## Ingredients

120g/4¼oz/1½ cups freshly grated wild
   horseradish roots (about 3–4 roots, depending
   on size foraged)
150ml/5fl oz/scant ⅔ cup apple cider vinegar
1 tsp salt

## Equipment

small preserving jar (about 250ml/9fl oz/
   generous 1 cup volume), sterilized

My favourite condiment of all time, it's perfect with venison, beef, beetroot and smoked fish. Whatever you do, don't mix it with yogurt, crème fraîche (sour cream) or double cream (heavy cream). You'll ruin the perfection you have created.

Wild horseradish packs a lot more intense heat than its cultivated cousins, so if you are using cultivated, just use a bit more. The volatile oil found in horseradish is called sinigrin and it can be highly irritating when cut or grated (see page 132 in the Plant Directory), so try not to get it in your eyes or nose. It does eventually evaporate, but can be very uncomfortable while it wears off.

## Method

Wash, scrub and peel the horseradish roots and, using a fine grater, grate the roots into a bowl until you have the desired amount.

Put the grated horseradish in the preserving jar, add the vinegar and salt and stir well. Put the lid tightly on the jar and leave it to rest in a cool, dark cupboard at room temperature for at least 1 week for the fermentation to take place, then store in the fridge. The horseradish sauce will keep for up to 6 months.

## WARNING

To prepare this amount of wild horseradish, I recommend working outside or in a well-ventilated area because once cut, wild horseradish can irritate the eyes and nose. Wear some kind of eye protection and try not to breathe in through your nose.

### TIP
*If you can't find wild horseradish, you can use two shop-bought horseradish roots instead.*

# BEETROOT & WILD HORSERADISH PUREE

The sweet, earthy notes of smoke-roasted beetroot (beets) in this puree help to mellow out the fire of the horseradish. It works really well with venison, pigeon, beef and smoked salmon. Use it as a side dish or pipe it onto canapés.

## Ingredients

5 beetroot (beets), trimmed
4 tbsp freshly grated wild horseradish
4 tbsp red wine vinegar
4 tbsp crème fraîche (sour cream)
salt and freshly ground black pepper

## Method

First, prepare to dirty cook the beetroot on hot coals by getting a good fire going (see page 34). Once your bed of embers is ready, put the beetroot in among the coals and cook for 30 minutes, turning occasionally, using tongs, until they have formed a fairly solid black crust all over. Remove them from the fire and leave to cool.

When cool enough to handle, simply crack the beetroot open, remove the beautifully cooked interior and put it in a blender along with the horseradish, vinegar, crème fraîche and 4 tablespoons of water. Season well with salt and pepper. Be generous with the black pepper because it really makes this puree.

Blend for 2–3 minutes until smooth, then adjust the seasoning, if necessary. Transfer the puree to a pan and heat it over a low heat until warm, then serve.

# STINGER NETTLE PESTO CAKES

These cakes were originally created as our 'veggie burger' for the occasional lost vegetarian who ended up in the Treehouse in search of enlightenment. The nettle is one of our finest wild plants, ridiculously available yet always underused. They have a flavour all of their own and can be used in the same way spinach is. If you are looking to harvest quite a few nettle tops, wear gloves. We all look fetching in a nice pair of pink or yellow ones and they never fail to add a bit of glamour to the hedgerows. If you do get stung, consider it payment for such a nutritious free green.

*Makes 8 cakes*

## Ingredients

200g/7oz/5 cups nettle tops
1 tbsp toasted hazelnuts or pine nuts
1 bunch of wild garlic (ramps) leaves, finely chopped, or 1 head of garlic, cloves separated, peeled and finely chopped
50g/1¾oz/⅔ cup panko breadcrumbs
40g/1½oz/½ cup grated Parmesan cheese
juice of ½ lemon
1 egg, beaten
salt and freshly ground black pepper
1 tbsp olive oil, for frying, plus extra for the burger mix, if needed
1 egg yolk, beaten, if needed

These can be served with just about anything, but they make a good base for meat or fish to sit on, and are especially good with rabbit – things that grow together almost certainly go together (see rabbit recipe on page 78).

## Method

Bring a large pan of water to the boil, add the nettles and simmer for 5 minutes until soft. Remove from the heat, drain in a colander and rinse with cold water to cool them. Using your hands, squeeze all the liquid from the nettles, remove any large stalks, then flatten the nettles out on a chopping board and chop finely until they have fluffed up, then put them in a mixing bowl.

Heat a frying pan over a high heat, add the hazelnuts and cook, stirring frequently, for 2–3 minutes until slightly coloured, then pound them in a pestle and mortar. Add the nuts to the nettles, along with the wild garlic, breadcrumbs, Parmesan, lemon juice and egg. Season generously with salt and pepper and mix well, using a fork.

Wet your hands with water to prevent the mixture from sticking to your hands, then shape the mixture into eight equal-sized cakes, giving it a squeeze to see if it holds. If it cracks, then the mix is too dry and you should add a little olive oil, or an egg yolk.

Reheat the frying pan over a high heat and add the oil. Add the cakes and fry for 2–3 minutes on each side until golden. Serve warm.

# BOURBON BACON JAM

Since its inception around 1500 BCE, bacon has been appreciated by kings and peasants alike. No one is too good for bacon, so why not turn it into jam?

## Ingredients

300g/10½oz pancetta lardons
3–4 shallots, peeled and finely chopped
4 garlic cloves, peeled and finely chopped
250ml/9fl oz/1 cup plus 2 tbsp strong black coffee
250ml/9fl oz/1 cup plus 2 tbsp apple cider vinegar
250g/9oz/1½ cups soft dark brown sugar,
   loosely packed
2 x 50ml/1¾oz/3 tbsp + 1 tsp shots of
   bourbon whisky

## Equipment

medium-sized preserving jar (about 500ml/
   17fl oz/2-cup volume), sterilized

This recipe is fairly quick and easy to make with a short list of ingredients. Ordinary smoked lardons will work just as well; try to chop them down if you can so they are well distributed in the end result. The bourbon really helps to add some depth of flavour and gives it an aged taste. The versatility of this jam is never ending and it works on so many levels, from topping burgers to spooning over poached eggs or even spreading it on toast. It is absolutely incredible.

## Method

Heat the lardons in a deep saucepan over a medium-high heat for 5–6 minutes to render the fat down and to get a bit of colour on them, then spoon the lardons onto a plate and set aside, leaving plenty of fat in the pan.

Reduce the heat to low and add the shallots and garlic to the fat. Cook them for 10–15 minutes, stirring occasionally, until they start to soften and caramelize.

Return the lardons to the pan along with the coffee, vinegar and sugar. Stir well, then cook over a medium heat for 35–45 minutes, stirring occasionally, until the liquid reduces and the consistency is thick and jam-like.

Spoon the bacon jam into a bowl and put the pan back on the heat. Pour one of the bourbon shots into the pan and, using a spatula, scrape the bottom of the pan to deglaze it. Make sure you get all that goodness stuck to the bottom of the pan and add it to the bowl of bacon jam. Stir well, then spoon the jam into a preserving jar and store in the fridge, where it will keep for up to 2 weeks.

Take the other shot of bourbon, raise the glass and smash it back in one, for you have just created one of the finest concoctions known to mankind. Well done. Find someone and give them a high five.

# PICKLES

Whether plant, mushroom, feather or fur, most of the ingredients we use at HGC come from the wild, so we are largely governed by the seasons. However, pickling is a vital part of what we do. While we like to showcase each season and try to only use what nature is providing at that very moment, pickling enables us to capture the flavours of other seasons and use them at another time of year.

## USEFUL WILDS TO PICKLE

Alexanders (buds, stems and flowers)

Blackberries (berries when they are green and also when ripe)

Burdock (roots)

Damson plum

Dandelion (buds and roots)

Douglas fir (use needles to make Douglas fir vinegar)

Elder (berries when they are still green and just turning purple)

Hogweed (buds, stems and flowers)

Horseradish (leaves and roots)

Mushrooms (trumpet chanterelles, hedgehog fungi and chanterelles)

Nettle (early spring or new-growth leaves)

Ox-eye daisy (buds)

Rocket (arugula) roots

Three-cornered leek (leaves, stems and flowers)

Wild garlic (ramps) (bulbs, leaves, scapes or buds, seed heads)

# HGC PICKLING LIQUID

This is basic but it has a wonderful balance of sugar to salt. We use a high-quality sea salt for the best flavour. You can add any spices or seasoning you wish to make it your own. We use this pickling liquid for everything, from wilds to carrots, beetroot (beets), beans, onions, cucumbers, chillies and cauliflowers.

## Method

Put all of the ingredients in a saucepan and heat over a medium heat, stirring continuously, for 1 minute until the sugar and salt have dissolved. Do not let the mixture boil. Remove the pan from the heat and set aside to cool completely before using.

*Makes 480ml/16¼fl oz/generous 2 cups*

## Ingredients

240ml/8fl oz/1 cup distilled white vinegar

240ml/8fl oz/1 cup water

3 tbsp granulated sugar

2 tbsp coarse sea salt

*TIP*

*Make sure to use the pickling liquid when it is cold. This will help the ingredients you're pickling to maintain their firm texture.*

# PICKLED CARROTS

These will keep for up to 3 months, if you don't plan to cook them. We mainly cook our pickles and find they're best within 2 days of pickling, before they've absorbed too much of the liquid. We take them out of the liquid, brush them with olive oil, then grill them over the fire for 3–4 minutes to get some colour on them and serve them 'al dente'. They work particularly well with rabbit.

## Ingredients

1 tbsp cumin seeds
450g/1lb baby carrots, trimmed and peeled
1 recipe quantity HGC Pickling Liquid
(see facing page)

## Equipment

medium-sized preserving jar (about
500ml/17fl oz/2-cup volume), sterilized

## Method

Heat a small frying pan over a medium-high heat. Add the cumin seeds and heat, stirring continuously, for 3–4 minutes until toasted and fragrant. Put the carrots in a medium-sized preserving jar, add the cumin seeds and cover with the pickling liquid. Cover tightly and store at room temperature.

# SMOKED PICKLED BEANS

These are very tasty little treats. They work well on a charcuterie board.

## Ingredients

200g/7oz untrimmed green beans
½ red chilli, finely sliced
1 recipe quantity cold HGC Pickling Liquid
(see facing page)

## Equipment

medium-sized preserving jar

## Method

Grill the green beans over a direct heat on the barbecue for 3–4 minutes until lightly charred. Remove from the heat and leave to cool. When cool, put them in a preserving jar, add the chilli and the cold pickling liquid, cover tightly and store at room temperature. They will be ready after 2 days, but taste best after a week.

# RESOURCES

The following list includes information I think you will find useful and suppliers that I wholeheartedly recommend. There are, of course, many other fantastic suppliers out there – just do the necessary research before you buy, and always buy the best quality you can afford.

### BASC (British Association for Shooting and Conservation)
*For all UK game-related information and DSC1 courses (Deer Stalking Certificate Level 1).*
basc.org.uk

### BDS (British Deer Society)
*For all UK deer-related information and DSC1 courses (Deer Stalking Certificate Level 1).*
bds.org.uk

### Blenheim Forge
*Beautiful handmade knives as well as custom projects.*
blenheimforge.co.uk

### Bush Gear
*Mora knives, firesteels and general outdoor kit.*
bushgear.co.uk

### Bushwear
*For game safe and all game larder equipment.*
bushwear.co.uk

### Country Fire Kitchen
*Asador frames, grills, planchas (griddles) and custom-made set-ups.*
countryfirekitchen.com

### Gransfors Bruks Axes
*Brilliant axes that come in an array of different sizes.*
gransforsbruk.com

### Hot Smoked
*For all your smoking needs, including barbecues, hot smokers, cold smoke generators, wood dust, smoking chips and accessories.*
hotsmoked.co.uk

### I.O. Shen Knives
*Fantastic range of knives for all occasions.*
ioshen.co.uk

### Kadai Firebowls
*Firebowls, tabletop grills, grill trays and all sorts.*
kadai.co.uk

### Netherton Foundry
*For all cast-iron and outdoor pots and pans.*
netherton-foundry.co.uk

### Oxford Charcoal
*Fantastic charcoal in an array of different flavours, from hardwood blends to single species and fruitwoods.*
oxfordcharcoal.co.uk

### Weber BBQs
*Amazing barbecues, from smokers to kettles and chimney starters, plus meat thermometers.*
weber.com

### Witloft
*Leather aprons for all your fire cookery needs and excellent knife rolls.*
witloft.com

# ABOUT THE AUTHOR

Nick Weston is a hunter, forager, fisherman and chef from Sussex in the UK. He left London after three years working as a freelance chef in the events industry and built a treehouse in a quiet Sussex wood from recycled and natural materials. For the following six months he lived in the woods completely off-grid to gain a better understanding of how to use wild ingredients by foraging, fishing and hunting for all his ingredients, supplemented by a few basic larder staples and a small vegetable patch. This provided him with a rich, varied diet and self-sufficient lifestyle, which would go on to form the ethos of Hunter Gather Cook. A book about his experience *The Tree House Diaries: How to Live Wild in the Woods* was published in 2010.

Hunter Gather Cook was established in March 2011 with the construction of the original HQ. Nick's vision was to create a foraging and cookery school that blended a mixture of foraging, game butchery and fire cookery with an emphasis on creating high-end dishes using wild produce. Several years on and many courses later Hunter Gather Cook has passed on their knowledge and skills to thousands of people with a passion for wild food and fire from their 9m (30ft) treehouse in the middle of the woods. Nick has continued to expand the wealth of courses they offer with the acquisition of an old threshing barn in a remote location at the foot of the South Downs, which is now the bricks and mortar of Hunter Gather Cook and houses all their new courses, banquets and events.

huntergathercook.com
Instagram: @huntergathercook

# INDEX

To place an order, contact:
GMC Publications Ltd, Castle Place,
166 High Street, Lewes, East Sussex,
BN7 1XU, United Kingdom.
Tel: +44 (0)1273 488005
www.gmcbooks.com